THE PARADOX OF THE WORLD

THE PARADOX

OF

THE WORLD

SERMONS

BY

JOHN OMAN, D.D.

CAMBRIDGE

AT THE UNIVERSITY PRESS

1921

CAMBRIDGE
UNIVERSITY PRESS

University Printing House, Cambridge CB2 8BS, United Kingdom

Cambridge University Press is part of the University of Cambridge.

It furthers the University's mission by disseminating knowledge in the pursuit of education, learning and research at the highest international levels of excellence.

www.cambridge.org
Information on this title: www.cambridge.org/9781107505278

© Cambridge University Press 1921

First published 1921
First paperback edition 2015

A catalogue record for this publication is available from the British Library

ISBN 978-1-107-50527-8 Paperback

ΣOÍ, ΓΝΉΣΙΑ ΣΎΖΥΓΕ

CONTENTS

I

THE SIGNS OF THE TIMES

MATTHEW xvi. 3. 'Ye know how to discern the face of the heaven; but ye cannot discern the signs of the times.'

OF the children of Issachar we are told in the Book of Chronicles that they had men of understanding of the times, to know what Israel ought to do. A tribe with this happy endowment among ourselves were greatly to be desired. We look to the tribe of the Churchmen or to the tribe of the Statesmen or to the tribe of the Pressmen; and when we fail to make discovery among any of them of this particular gift of producing leaders, we consider the matter at an end. But there is an old saying, 'Like people, like priest,' which means, we must deserve good leaders, before we have a right to expect them. Issachar's striking success in this supremely valuable sphere of production cannot have been mere accidental fortune in the birth of genius, but must have been due to an unusual intentness in the whole tribe upon being rightly and not merely pleasantly guided. Real leaders are not discoverable till first we believe in that alone which can lead them, even in truth and righteousness.

Great leaders are no doubt a gift of God, yet, even if God did send them, they can grow only on the soil of the common wisdom. Great men may have extended powers of applying wisdom, but wisdom itself is not confined to genius specially endowed, for, unless it is a common possession, the conspicuous manifestation of it will merely be rejected as conspicuous folly.

In the Bible wisdom is the one genuine hall-mark of all really spiritual persons. To be spiritual is just to be able to penetrate to the inner meaning of events and know the right principles on which to judge them. The task no doubt is high, but, undertaken in the right way, it is not difficult. The moral weather, our Lord here says, is as easy to foretell as the material, did we with the same sincerity apply our experience to reading its signs. Failure is not due to lack of ability, learning or practical talent, but to bias of the will away from the determination to know what is to be, towards what we should like to be, and from patience in interpreting signs, towards a hasty response to mere impressions.

1. It is an affair of sincerity

If we set out on our task as hypocrites whose purpose is to discover what they like and persuade themselves of what they wish to believe, and not as sincere persons with the simple resolve to know what God wills and the reality of the situation determines, a right result is hopeless from the beginning.

Though the words 'Ye hypocrites' are not found in the correct text of Matthew, they are found in the corresponding passage of Luke, and, in Matthew, 'a wicked and adulterous generation seeking after a sign' has the same meaning. The point of the saying is that the sole difficulty in judging is the insincerity of our souls. Not as we are learned or astute or practical, but as we are sincere, have we discernment of the spiritual forces and fore-knowledge of their issues.

Hypocrisies are of all shades, from conscious acting to unconscious bias, and have all kinds of manifestations, from ostentatious religious profession to ostentatious superiority to all religion. The Pharisees prayed in public and robbed widows' houses, and with the same punctilious regard to legal form in both actions. Religious observances are not in such repute at present that temptation should lie in this particular direction. But oratory on social regeneration and the brotherhood of man, with merely rhetorical application to things at large, without affecting more than the barest legal recognition of their rights in dealings with actual people, does as well. Fluency on platforms and conspicuousness at demonstrations, unaccompanied by humble and unselfish service, will make just as impossible any discovery that a system may have private profit in it, yet be full of reasons for foreboding evil, as any kind of religious parade.

Nor is this the only way of being far from sincerity.

Our Lord said men sought to kill Him, not because they thought what He said false, but because they knew it to be true. And for no other reason can anger be vehement and enduring. What we know to be false must seem to us too certain to fail of itself in the end for us to entertain towards it murderous hatred. But if we suspect that what we hate may be true, while this way of lynching may seem too crude, we shall be found in some way trying to kill the soul of its truth. The way may be less brutal without being less fatal. The reformer who means business can be silenced without either amending the evil he denounces or cutting his throat: for there are all kinds of ways of making it unhappy for your prophets when they refuse to prophesy smooth things to you.

A great deal of human nature showed itself in Ahab, when, after insisting that Micaiah should tell him the whole naked truth, he put the prophet on bread and water of affliction for uttering anything so unpleasant. That old simple way of sending to prison now needs more troublesome formalities, even in these days when it is again more available. But there are other ways of prescribing to Micaiah's habit of mind discipline in diet. It may be a little more roundabout to starve him by only listening to sermons and reading books and applauding speeches and buying newspapers which echo our own preferences and prejudices, and shunning all that declare naked, painful truth. But it is quite as effective.

Thus the pulpit, the platform and the press are tuned by the same old method of food control—and the pulpit not least. The demand for smooth things has been vocal as well as insistent, and sometimes this has been directly backed, with an autocracy worthy of Ahab, by loss of place and pay. On the other side, it is made plain to men that, if they will show the consolations of Christ to abound, without insisting that they are chiefly for wounds received in spiritual conflict, and if they will esteem decent behaviour quite sufficient enduring of hardness, and stir no more than a sentimental feeling for those from whom God has withheld prosperity, which is to be regarded as the supreme mark of His esteem, and not make love all a matter of humble fellowship and measureless service, their pews will be filled, their circulation enormous, their popularity great, and their pay not altogether grudging. But if they, in Christ's name, insist that the world should be turned upside down and that, with the present idolatries, the sword will reach even to the life, so making religion searching and revolutionary and not wholly safe and easy and comforting, well, it is always possible to ignore them and to hope they will manage to exist long enough on bread and water of affliction to see the folly of their croaking as we return in health and triumph. In that mood also we are not of much value as prophets of our time or even for discovering men of understanding who know what Israel ought to do.

But we may have a much higher devotion to truth, yet fail to read the signs of the times with utter sincerity. You say, 'I will hear what God the Lord will speak,' and you are tolerant of those who say, He will speak peace to his people only if they do not turn again to folly. But is there not a quiet assumption that, in your own case, certain privileges at least must be exempt, and following Christ cannot have quite the old hard conditions or your cross ever prove an agony and not an ornament upon your shoulder?

Wherefore, none of us can altogether acquit ourselves of being so involved in an idolatrous and self-indulgent world that we are unable to read aright its signs. No right understanding of the troubled age on which we have fallen will be given us till we cease to measure God's reality by our liking and lay ourselves wholly open to be taught His purpose, however hostile to our desires, however hard for our ears to hear and our hearts to receive; and, not till then, can we have understanding of our times to know what our Israel ought to do.

2. IT IS AN AFFAIR OF SIGNS

The first requirement of conscientiousness is to be earnest in discovering God's view. But there is a kind of conscientiousness which is satisfied with merely removing doubts about our own views. The perplexing and inadequate result would make us more distrustful of its guidance did we realise that only an earnestness rightly directed is truly conscientious. If the record which the Apostle bears to the Jews, that they have a zeal, but not according to knowledge, is praise, it is very faint praise, for a zeal unconcerned about discovering its true direction is not occupied in the patient search for reality, but is still a very disastrous kind of hypocrisy.

True sincerity is not a mere emotional response to impressions, but puts all its mind, as well as all its heart, into interpreting signs.

Have you ever seen an old fisherman studying the weather before committing his frail barque to the mercy of the sea? I think of one who for seventy years had braved the Atlantic, of how his long-sighted grey eyes used to search the horizon on a doubtful morning, and of the long experience behind them by which he interpreted every wisp of cloud and every shimmer of sunshine. To go out in good weather was a necessity of daily bread; to be out in bad might mean a watery grave. Many he had known who, having misread the signs of the sky, had gone out and never returned. Superficial impression, therefore, had no weight with him, but only the experience he had won at no less risk than his life, and which, misapplied, might cost the lives of others as well as his own.

More often we interpret the signs of the time like children examining the sky on the morning of a picnic. Their one anxiety is to be allowed to go, and any brightness impresses them, and beyond impression they do not travel. For that, nothing is more effective than the high and lurid red of the dawn, and it leaves them no ear for the voice of experience which interprets it as the sign of foul weather.

By this hasty response to mere impression, simple truth is miscalled simplicity, confident assertion knowledge, cleverness insight, pose strength, outward accord with accepted standards goodness, material success life's real triumph.

Those who are thus guided by first impressions experience cannot teach. Nothing will alter their conviction that an easy prosperity, at least if won without absolute wrong-doing, is life's supreme security, and poverty, even strenuous poverty, its chief uncertainty and limitation. They may know many who are happy without wealth and many who have sold happiness for it, but it makes no impression and raises no question. Still less do they ever reflect on how history tells us that scarcely ever, in the long history of the race, have the greatest and best ever lived in great abundance or ever found poverty a hindrance.

Even when men turn from life's highest calls and subject their souls to a dull routine worldliness for their families rather than for themselves, how often does their labour go astray! Excessive diligence in making for their children material provision proves the poorest substitute for being their true friend in learning wisdom and steadfastness of purpose and clear moral vision and a sense of responsibility and all that could make their time on earth safe and blessed in noble service for lofty ends. Someone has called the young people who have been thus well equipped for self-indulgence and ill equipped for self-discipline the dangerous classes; and for those who could read aright, there was perhaps no more ominous sign of the time than the increase of their number by our long prosperity. Even now many are hoping against hope that the War will somehow end so that a luxurious prosperity may be more increased than ever before.

If we, however, can discern the signs of the time at all, God meaneth not so, but has in store for most of us the discipline of fewer possessions and higher demands. So long as men are guided merely by what is visibly impressive, their judgment of things, and still more of men, becomes appallingly immediate and superficial. Especially the power is lost of distinguishing in work and character the calm glow of evening after the long day of labour and thought, from the crude and glaring red of morning while ignorance is still self-confident and character not yet proved. Cleverness serves for solid thinking, good form for moral insight, response to the influences around for fixed principle, and geniality of disposition for high character. Yet these are the grand distinctions which ultimately decide all destinies. The result is that men can no longer discriminate between first-hand experience and the multiplication of echoes. Thereupon they think the future can be decided by votes, whether cast for

God's reality or against it, and measure prosperity by money and not by men, and seek to arrive by haste and not by patience.

Though they may still be serious in seeking physicians for their bodies, their habit of mind betrays them even there into being more impressed by an agreeable bedside manner, than by knowledge and skill. But physicians for their souls they choose wholly by bedside manner and the sweetness of their physic, with positive disapprobation for the power to diagnose and heal the disease. There is no insight to discern prophets, who, because they will penetrate beyond impressions and interpret the signs of God's real purpose with the world, and, because they will only speak what they themselves have seen, enter life grey and sombre, with heavy mists of troubled thought and perplexed experience upon their souls and upon their speech. There is no eye to mark the upward movement which promises a wide heaven and a clear earth in time. Instead, cheap and fluent pleasantness of speech and pretty fancies, picturesque quotations for form, and clever manipulation of secondhand experience for substance are the acme of excellence.

If only it glow, there is no concern to inquire whether it be with the evening red of grave eloquence, after serious reflection and deep experience, or with the mere morning red of flashy rhetoric and confident assertion. Then the future is estimated by the hope of pleasure and reputation and possession, and the only forces that can be seen at work in the world are loud and masterful and of visible organisation; and men judge as we should judge a tree by its abundant leaf, without any eye for the unobtrusive stain which creeps up its trunk signifying death. The sign of a dying soul is hard selfishness, with all its ideals being eaten into by indulgence, and the signs of a dying society are blind rivalry for wealth, the extending stain of impurity, the need of shallow excitement and concentration on fleeting pleasures.

In the last resort the issue is religious. The true sign of the times is not our possessions, not even our doings, not even our visible moralities, but our faiths. If the certain future is according to God's purpose, we can only know it as we believe in the forces with which God works.

The prophets saw ominous signs in crooked policies, public and private injustice, and still more in heartless luxury and unbridled lust and low pleasures which culminated in drunkenness. But, when they went to the root of the matter, they came to a religion which performed rituals, but did not humble and cleanse the soul; which would persuade God with gifts to give men their desires and be on their side, but did not do justice and love mercy and walk humbly with its God. The worst sign of a time is the absence of all religion, but the presence of a religion occupied with impressions and not with signs, with immediate success and not with the real faiths of the heart, is scarcely less ominous.

In a Church, making the study of impressiveness its first concern, thinking, not in terms of a reverence which humbles the soul, but of a ritual which gratifies the senses, of a preaching which pleases the ear and stirs barren emotion without requiring a penitence which cleanses the heart and a love which claims the service of all we are and all we have, of institutions and numbers and prestige which require no going to Christ without the camp of social approval and accepted opinion, we have the most ominous of all forms of organised hypocrisy. Our Lord found it in His day, and thought it the mere lowering red of the morning, a portent of approaching tornado. When 'trampling God's courts' is mistaken for worship, absence of denial for living faith, outward decency of behaviour for goodness of the heart, timid regard for consequences and human disapproval for consecration to righteousness and reverence for the judgment of God, and unquestioning acceptance of tradition for the knowledge of God, all will seem well to those who judge by impressions, and all will seem ominous of disaster to those who interpret the signs of the times.

Already the morning red is dying out into foul weather. Even the low measure of religion which is embodied in customary worship, traditional faith and negative morality, is no longer being maintained. In the storm that is upon us, it is plain that all but the truth men have themselves seen and the good their own hearts have chosen is going by the board. The common idea of strengthening the things that remain is a more studied and organised appeal to impressiveness—vaster religious institutions, more united effort, more vehement affirmation, more elaborate ritual, more methodical moulding of the mind of the young, more systematised emotional appeal to the unthinking. But what will it do to avert the real spiritual disaster, which is also ominous of all other disasters, which is that, as the world is thought to be our sole good, Christianity is regarded as a dead issue? What will save us except the resolute purpose to get down to our Lord's demand, to read the signs of our times simply by utter sincerity, and to affirm no truth we have not seen, to persuade to nothing of which we are not ourselves persuaded, and to trust no other appeal except the evidence of the truth itself to the minds that see it, and to offer no good except what our hearts have chosen and our lives are serving, and to offer it only on the same exclusive and austere conditions?

The morning red of impressiveness we cannot recover, or, if we did, it would only be a fitful glow, the forerunner of even fouler weather; and we can look forward to the promise of the calm afterglow only through a long day of earnest thought and steadfast patience and resolute purpose to hear only what God will speak, and of learning of His ways by unswerving loyalty to His will. Religion has only one imperious demand—utter sincerity in our thinking and feeling and acting. The lack of it is the supreme sign of disaster, the presence of it the one promise of a right use of this life, as well as of any higher fulfilment of it in the life to come. But we are sincere only as we pass beyond all that merely impresses, to the signs of our real moral and spiritual state, to the signs of the supreme and final realities by which all our futures are ultimately determined.

II

A DYING CIVILISATION

I Kings xix. 12. 'And after the fire a still small voice.'

The sublimity of this scene should impress us with its tremendous significance, but, as we watch the haggard solitary figure at the mouth of the cave, the shattered head of Horeb towering above him, and the desert stretching out dim and boundless and desolate before, and hear the rocks crash in tornado, and feel the earth quake in pent-up agony, and see the lightning wrap the world in flame, and shudder with awe as the tumult of nature changes to the sudden silence of the great waste places of the earth, our imagination is so filled with the spectacle that we may forget to ask what it meant for that lone watcher.

Positive misunderstanding, moreover, is introduced by the translation of our text as 'a still small voice,' and especially by the accepted exposition of it both in preaching and poetry. The tumult in which God was not is taken to be the vehement methods of judgment, and in particular Elijah's violence with idolatry and the priests of Baal. The 'still small voice,' in which God was, is then a declaration of the gentle ways of God and a prophecy of Him who was full of grace and truth.

But even Christ's denunciation of an adulterous

generation, who corrupted religion by hypocrisy, could be heart-shaking as earthquake and scathing as lightning; and no one ever announced more terrible judgments. Besides, if this voice rebuked violence and promised gentleness, why should it be followed by the announcement of just such a terrible upheaval in human society as had passed over nature? Why was Elijah to anoint Hazael to be king over Syria, and Jehu to be king over Israel, and Elisha to be prophet in his own room, that him who escaped from the sword of Hazael, Jehu should slay, and him who escaped from the sword of Jehu, Elisha should slay? Instead of gentleness and rebuke of the spirit of judgment, the doom is so appalling that Elijah himself, for all his sternness, sought delay when he took the first step of calling Elisha, and Elisha wept in the streets of Damascus when he took the second by appointing the kingdom to Hazael.

The seven thousand who have not bowed the knee to Baal are the one hope in the distress. They become the holy remnant from which is to spring a new nation, and then the servant of the Lord who is to be a light to lighten the Gentiles as well as the glory of Israel. But even their presence, though it assures hope at the end of the day, cannot avert judgment or do more than delay the blotting-out of civilisation. And it is this blotting-out which is predicted in the solemn stillness which follows the agony of nature.

The only doubtful word is that translated 'small.'
Literally it means something beaten fine like dust,
but it was also in common use for something thin
like a veil. The rest is in no way doubtful. It is
not a still voice, but a voice of silence. The silence
itself speaks as when the heavens, which have no
speech or language, declare the glory of God. The
best commentary is the passage in Job, where
Eliphaz says that, in visions of the night, a mysterious
presence passed before his face, and a voice of
silence—not a voice following silence, but the voice
of the silence itself—said, Can man be pure before
God who charges even His angels with folly? Our
text, therefore, means a voice of a silence which
either wrapped the world like a veil or fell upon it
like dust on one vast desolation. In either case it
means the arresting, solemn, dread stillness of the
great waste-places. It speaks in the same language
of nature as the tornado, the earthquake and the
lightning. As they meant invasion, revolution and
moral disaster, this typifies the ruined world which
shall remain when the work, of which Hazael, Jehu
and Elisha are but the beginnings, has reached its
calamitous close.

That the Lord was not in tempest, earthquake
or fire, does not mean that they were contrary to
His mind or apart from His purpose, or even that
he did not command them into action, but only
that the prophet could not yet hear in them the
deliverance he expected, the satisfaction of his

longing for a purified religion and a regenerated society. That first spoke in the voice of the arresting silence which fell upon the lightning-riven masses of Horeb and the storm-driven sands of the far-stretching desert. This desolate stillness first uttered to his heart the hope that, as once the religion of Israel had been cleansed of idolatries and its society ordered on simple human relations in the wilderness, so it might be again.

By invasion, insurrection and moral corruption the present civilisation would fall to ruin. Its worldly and selfish prosperity, which drowned every voice of the human heart except ambition and pride of place and love of pleasure and greed of gain and all-devouring lust, would cease; its worship, which debased religion to ceremonial and faith to super-stition, would sink into silence. Then, in that dread stillness of desolation, man would once again hear the deep divine voices in his own heart, love his neighbour in justice and kindness, and worship God in simplicity and humility. Then, too, above all, the seven thousand who had not bowed the knee to Baal would come to their own, and in God's name rebuild a new and better world.

This was the prophet's hope: and, without hope, he was not asked to do his work. But, so far is his resistance to evil from being rebuked, that he is ordered to begin an upheaval which would shake all false securities, burst all unreal bonds, and manifest the disaster of all corruptions. In spite of the hope shining at the end, this way of the wilderness remained dark and terrible, a way before which even Elijah's high courage quailed and his stern heart melted. The silence of desolation, which followed tempest and earthquake and fire, meant the blotting out of civilisation by brutal wars of conquest, by national anarchies and by moral corruptions; and no vision behind it of religious or social regeneration could change the awful doom of misery, captivity, slaughter, which overshadowed men and women and even little children. Beyond lay the vision of God's Holy Mountain where the ransomed of the Lord should walk and none hurt or destroy, but even that hope could not still the present agony which rent the heart of every prophet, till he cried 'O Lord, how long?' nor did it alter the terrible answer, 'Until cities be waste without inhabitants and houses without men, and the land become utterly waste.'

In that voice of the silence of desolation can be heard the whole burden of Hebrew prophecy. Even Isaiah and Jeremiah, for all their far greater gifts of genius, are but followers and disciples of Elijah, and only the scope and splendour of their application obscures the extent to which they merely re-echo this message of the voices of the desert.

Elijah, listening in trembling awe to this pause of the utter, lone silence of the waste, learned the measure of value which gave birth to all the prophets' thoughts of God as ruling in righteousness the armies of Heaven as well as the inhabitants of Earth.

From it they learned that no interests compare with
the interests of the soul, that every loss is gain upon
which the soul can feed, and that earthly kingdoms
are less than nothing and vanity when God's Kingdom is at stake. Their sublime monotheism, with
all its confidence in the wise omnipotent righteous
sovereignty of the One God, is just the application
of this discovery. God has ceased to be an idol to
secure individual prosperity or a national deity to
guarantee His people's security, and has become
the director of all destinies and the measure of all
good, for whose ends man might with profit suffer
and die and the world with advantage be reduced
to ruin and desolation. Though this message never
ceases to be tremendous and appalling, all true
thoughts, not only of God's righteous sovereignty,
but of His patient wise love, spring from it. And,
if it grow only on soil ploughed deep with the agony
of men and nations, it bears, as no other plant, the
fruit of eternal hope.

This we see in all the prophets from Amos to
Jeremiah.

The work of Amos is so amazingly original, that
it has been described as the most remarkable pheno-
menon in the history of the human spirit, yet the
heart of his message is just what Elijah saw at
Horeb: and his continual reference to fire seems to
show that he was not ignorant of his dependence.
God will send His fire upon Syria, which is still to
him the house of Hazael, and upon Israel and Judah

and all the nations round about. And fire means with Amos also the consuming power of the moral nature of things when ignored and defied. The present civilisation is doomed, and nothing in it more certainly than its religion of much ritual and little righteousness. God despises its feasts, has no delight in its solemn assemblies, and pays no regard to its sacrifices, which were never offered in the wilderness.

This is his only reference to the wilderness, yet it is of deep significance, as it plainly hints that there alone lies the hope of a purified, sincere and neighbourly piety. But of the coming desolation which was to reduce religion to this simplicity, nowhere are there more terrible descriptions. There may even be a definite reference to the experience of Elijah in the demand for silence after the songs of the Temple have become howlings and the dead are too many and the living too few for the rites of burial. Even of the remnant he can only say that their wisdom is in silence, and that, if they hate the evil and love the good and establish judgment in the gate, it may be that God will be gracious unto them. The hymn of restoration at the close, when cities should be rebuilt and inhabited, and fields sown and the bread eaten, and vineyards and gardens planted and the wine drunk and the fruit enjoyed, is thought to be later, but, as it is a hope still limited to Israel, it may not; and, in any case, we cannot suppose that Amos, any more than Elijah, was asked to prophesy mere desolation without some assurance that God's voice spoke in its silence, promising a purer religion and a regenerated society.

Invasion and insurrection are for Amos, as for Elijah, the means of destruction. Yet they remain vague hints of slaughter and wasting and captivity and risings against the house of Jeroboam, the descendant of Jehu. Only when we come to the supreme destructive force, the nature of moral reality, have we a concreteness, an intensity, an inevitableness, without parallel. A nation in which lies are cherished and prophets silenced, the needy robbed and the meek oppressed, adultery flagrant and drunkenness rampant, luxury rapacious, recreation frivolous and amusement the only serious pursuit, till nothing is left sacred, God calls to contend with fire not to be escaped in heaven or hell or the depths of the sea, till the land shall melt and its inhabitants mourn.

In Hosea there is a still clearer conception that the goal is the wilderness. 'Behold, I will allure her and bring her into the wilderness, and speak comfortably unto her. And I will give her her vineyards from thence, and the Valley of Troubling for a door of hope.' Anarchy is already doing its destructive work within and the invader is thundering at the gate. But the inevitable still lies in the moral and spiritual forces. A nation sunk in idolatry, licentiousness, intemperance, greed, pride and injustice, cannot abide.

A great agony of sympathy possesses the heart

of the prophet. But comfort springs from the very depth of his woe, for the very agony in his own heart interprets the heart of God. 'In Him the fatherless findeth mercy,' 'His heart is turned within Him,' 'His compassions are kindled together,' He cannot finally give up His people.

The message of Isaiah is not essentially different. Though the destruction of Judah is deferred, the present civilisation is doomed in every nation. And the powers before which it is to fall are still the same. First there is conquest. Assyria is at hand, a razor Judah herself has hired, which will shave her bare. Next there is anarchy. 'Children are their princes, and babes rule over them,' and the distress is so great that anyone with clothing is urged to be a ruler and take in hand to bring some order into the ruin.

But the final, the unescapable cause of disaster is still that, however it be ignored or denied, the supreme reality is moral and spiritual. A nation cannot abide when religion degenerates into complicated ceremonial, trampling of God's courts, presenting vain oblations and calling solemn assemblies, when the heart's best reverence is so material that it cannot rise above superstition and idolatry, when pride flaunts its luxury in the face of poverty, and wealth won by oppression is spent in strong drink and frivolous and licentious festivities. This is the all-consuming fire in which men shall be 'devoured like stubble and their blossom go up like dust.'

At the end lies still the discipline of the wilderness. The land is to be a place of briars and thorns where the sparse inhabitants hunt and dig and pasture their few cattle for the simplest livelihood.

Yet in this stock of a felled tree, the holy remnant, as Isaiah names the seven thousand who have not bowed the knee to Baal, are the life out of which there will be a growth more spacious and glorious, an Israel of a faith and a righteousness which will show that great is the Holy One of Israel in the midst of her.

Later there was a change to a larger, more gracious, more spiritual conception of the work of the holy remnant. From a mere seed from which might grow a renovated Israel, it came to be a re-deeming leaven in the whole world, through whom the knowledge of the Lord should cover the earth as the waters cover the sea, from whose pure and sincere worship would proceed the law which would establish perfect peace in perfect righteousness, not by any form of outward compulsion, but by the covenant of a new spirit within of truth and love.

Even more pointedly and exclusively this message of the wilderness was the prophetic burden of Jeremiah; while, through him, the method of the remnant was still clearly conceived as service and sacrifice.

Finally, under his influence, the remnant came to be later the Suffering Servant, whose work crowned the prophetic hope of the Old Testament and was the supreme preparation for Him who came from the bosom of the Father to declare Him and establish among men the Kingdom of Heaven.

The Old Testament has become in these days a real, an appallingly real book, and no part of it more concerns us than this central message of the silence of desolation.

When there is no principle of righteousness to oppose to the brutal strength of invasion, no rule of duty and devotion to maintain civil order, no worship but of place and gain and pleasure to give regard for man made in God's image and reverence for the soul which is His breath in our mortal clay, the spirit is dead and only the pampered body remains and there is no need to ask,

> Shall worms inheritors of this excess
> Eat up thy charge?

Then the only hope remaining is that 'the soul may live upon its servant's loss.'

When the great gift of civilisation, so rich in its possibilities for higher thought and purer worship, for gracious sympathies and helpful, brotherly human relations, is misused for obscuring the vital demands of religion, for enriching the rich and impoverishing the poor, for competition in which strength serves only selfish desire, and for a measure of values by wealth and not by worth and wisdom and goodness, there is no hope but in its destruction and a return to the solemn stillness of the wilderness

where men may hear, in the deeper voices of their
own hearts, the call of the Divine Will of righteousness and love above them and of the sacred humanities
around them.

We have often said there are worse things than
war; and, in spite of all these recent years have
taught us of its horrors, it is still true that there
are subjections and disloyalties worse than war.
Yet war, not to bring nations to their senses that
we may once again trust the securities of reason
and righteousness, but to put each other in strait-
waistcoats of annexations and armed suppressions
and control of material resources, is only what the
ancient peoples like Assyria attempted to do by
humiliating subjection and crushing tribute and the
removing of peoples. The result could only be once
again to turn the world into a permanent Bedlam
in which civilisation would end in mutual destruction.

Nor could we save anything out of the ruin
except by having in us a principle of reasonableness
and righteousness and unselfish regard for human
good which, by right of its own nature, could appeal
against mad ambition and brutal aggression.

With even more confidence we can say there are
worse things than insurrection. Our own civil wars
have won for us more permanent good than our
many foreign wars: and even the chaos and weakness
of Russia might be a cheap price for an enlightened
and just and ordered freedom. Something of revolution, if not by arms, yet by other ways of anarchy,

every country in Europe may soon have to face. But again how much of our civilisation we can bring out of it will depend on the measure of responsibility and devotion to liberty, for the growth of man's spirit and not for unbridled ambition and material good, we can oppose to the excesses of license and personal ambition.

But the heart-shaking part of this ancient message of the silence of the wilderness is that there are worse things even than the blotting out of our whole civilisation in war and anarchy. Terrible as that would be, it is better than to pamper the body and starve the spirit, to make machines of men and blot out human kindness, to find our heaven in the world and shut out God. Civilisation is a great good, and no prophet despises even its material blessings or ceases to hope for their return when men shall have discovered that prosperity is not a god to be worshipped, but only a means of worshipping God through using it to serve the noblest welfare of His children. Yet civilisation is no end in itself, but, on the contrary, a civilisation, without justice and mercy, without purity and self-control, without reverence for truth and beauty and goodness, without a sense for things unseen and eternal, without a religion that passes by observances and activities and offerings to do justly and love mercy and walk humbly with our God, is the supreme obstacle to God's purpose with the spirit of man, and the supreme denial of His eternal Rule of Truth and Love.

However appalling the agony, God will not hesitate to destroy it, nay, He has so made the world and the moral nature of things, that it is necessarily self-destructive, as, for the final good, every corrupt thing always is. Our present calamity may be great, yet to leave us in a state in which the world was our god and we had our selfish desires, but had leanness in our souls, would have been a still greater disaster, for it would have meant that God had renounced His high task with the world and the spirit of man.

As of old salvation can only come through the holy remnant. To it we belong as we do not bow the knee to the Baal of worldly success and lust of pleasure and power, but worship the Father in spirit and in truth by reverencing only what is spiritual and true.

Our first task is to save what we can of our present world by the call to sincere penitence and simple faith. But it may be that we shall not be heard till the striving and crying of a complex, worldly, prosperous age have fallen silent. Then our value for rebuilding our waste civilisation to the true glory of God and the real good of man will depend on the measure we have been, like Isaiah and the children that God had given him, for signs and for wonders, in our unfaltering faith that God does not fail and is not discouraged, and in our possession of the prophetic vision which sees through all the night of darkness and distress 'the new heavens and the new earth wherein dwelleth righteousness.' Then so high will the destiny of man appear and so glorious God's final kingdom of peace established in truth and righteousness, that we shall know, how, throughout all the terrible journey towards it, 'in all our affliction He was afflicted, and the angel of His presence saved us: in His love and in His pity He redeemed us: and He bare us and carried us all the days of old.'

III

GOD'S INSTRUMENT AND GOD'S AGENT

2 Kings viii. 11. 'And he settled his countenance stedfastly upon
   him, until he was ashamed: and the man of God wept.'

ALL of us alike are God's instruments. By no setting
of our hearts on wickedness or doing evil with both
our hands can we prevent God from using us. Our
folly will serve Him, when our wisdom fails; our
wrath praise Him, though our wills rebel. Yet,
as God's instruments without intention and in our
own despite, we generally serve God's ends only as
we defeat our own. To be God's agent is quite
another matter. This we are only as we learn God's
will, respond to His call, work faithfully together
with Him, and find our own highest ends in fulfilling His.

But while the mere instrument is constantly
broken and cast aside that God's work may proceed,
the true good of His agent is itself of the essence
of God's purpose.

In Hazael and Elisha, as they stand looking into
each other's eyes in that narrow ancient street, this
contrast between God's blind, unwilling tool and
His conscious, consecrated fellow-worker is incarnate. We should consider them well, for both the
use we shall make of life, and the use life will make

of us, depend entirely on whether we are of Hazael's kin or of Elisha's.

1. LET US LOOK AT GOD'S INSTRUMENT

You see the first minister of state, arrayed in oriental magnificence of office, with many gorgeous attendants in his train avouching his dignity, a channel of gifts beyond the dreams of avarice, the wielder of every power short of the sceptre, and of that also by the trust and favour of the king, with a renown which busy rumour has carried even to the prophet in hostile Israel.

Hazael's abilities, moreover, are equal to his position and reputation. Especially he has imagination, the pre-eminent gift for greatness, without which no man has royalty of nature for true distinction in any sphere, but carries even riches and position and renown as a mere ass's burden. Imagination gives Hazael soaring ambition, and, what is more, munificence in things material and penetration into human qualities as wings to sustain its flight. The order to take a present in his hand expands into forty camels' load of all the good things of Damascus: and, the moment he sees Elisha, he is aware that this lavishness is not a whit overdone. He does not judge, like the children in Israel, by the cut of the hair or the fashion of the clothes, but discerns in that plain travel-stained civilian the biggest man he had ever met, a man to be addressed as, 'My Lord,' a man to whom nothing less than a lordly present could be offered, and one well worth winning at the price.

Nor is that all. The imagination of this Macbeth of Damascus is more stirred by the unseen than by the seen. A supernatural suggestion of his destiny means more to him than the possession of an army. It plays the part with him of the witches' prophecy with Macbeth, assuring to him:

> The golden round
> Which fate and metaphysical aid doth seem
> To have thee crown'd withal.

Only the small and shallow man thinks he drives the chariot of the universe. What Goethe has called the demonic element in every really great man is, on the contrary, the sense of being a child of destiny. Though from men neither reverent nor scrupulous, Caesar's assurance in the storm, "You carry Caesar and his fortunes," and Napoleon's cry, "The world still turns for us," when the armies of Europe were hemming him in after the Russian disaster, have something akin to the religious assurance of a devout Calvinist like Cromwell. Nor can a man move the world with ideas any more than with deeds, without some sense, like the Apostle, of being consecrated to it from his mother's womb.

Thus the world saw Hazael: and was it not right in thinking him a man to command the uses of the present and control the issues of the future?

But Elisha showed himself truly a man of God

both by looking deeper into Hazael's heart and surprising there a guilty secret, which made himself weep and even this man of blood and iron look down ashamed before his steadfast gaze, and by looking farther into his fortunes and seeing the vanity of its gains when all should be weighed.

Three marks of God's mere instrument Elisha discerned.

First, there was *unbridled ambition,* not less evident for a submissive bearing and a lowly speech. When Elisha tells of coming greatness, he knows he is only giving utterance to Hazael's own mind; and when Hazael replies, 'What is thy servant?,' the obeisance does not hide the thought that even the royal position and the most extended sway are no more than his desert.

No driving force more ensures success than such vast ambition, even though it be the supreme denial of God's requirement of a humble mind in His children. And—what may seem still stranger in God's world—its success God often puts to great uses. Alexander's ambition of conquest spread the Greek language and Greek ideas for the progress of the world and the preparation for Christianity; Caesar's ambition imposed a peace upon the world, under which knowledge spread, and peaceful commerce united the peoples, and a higher religion secured a footing in the earth; Napoleon's ambition ended many grave oppressions, emancipating a large part of Europe from serfdom, and ultimately forwarded both freedom and equal law. And that remains true, though the misery for others and the fleeting profit for themselves justify Pascal's sarcastic estimate of the folly of swaggering about conquering the world, as excusable for a crude youth like Alexander, but unpardonable frivolity in a sensible middle-aged man like Caesar. The gain of the present ambition which is now blotting-out humanity is still beyond our vision, and the loss and suffering visible to the blindest, but we can still trust that God does not faint and is not discouraged, and that out of it He will bring something worthy of our distress, even while the ambitions themselves prove, as of old, self-destructive.

In humbler spheres also, though, so far as its own true place and abiding possession is concerned,

> Vaulting ambition o'erleaps its selle
> And falls on th' other—,

it is constantly an instrument of God for enriching life by discoveries and achievements which for no love of good its possessor ever had in his heart would he have pursued. While only by right motive does God estimate any man's good, the worst motive does not prevent God from using men for His own higher ends.

Second, you see *atrocious cruelty*. Hazael's ambition is not qualified by any illusion about the beneficence of his reign. Though the picture Elisha drew of the misery he was to work might have touched the hardest heart, when Hazael understood that he occupied the centre of the scene as a great conqueror, he cried, 'But what is thy servant, who is but a dog, that he should do this great thing!' Cruelty for him was the equivalent of glory, and blood and tears the measure of renown.

The story of human cruelty is an appalling record. How often has the conqueror repeated the work of Hazael, consuming towns with fire, slaying young men, dashing little ones in pieces, ripping up women with child. We dreamt that the heart of man had grown incapable of such iniquity: and now even that is beyond our dreaming. We may wonder if it be not capable still of inventing instruments of torture, and, like the Inquisition, attempting again to extend empire, by cruelty, from the body to the mind.

Yet even cruelty God may turn to His own ends. Though still harder to accept than His use of ambition, without a trust that God has a purpose He can make it serve, human cruelty dethrones for us either God's goodness or His omnipotence; and one is a mockery without the other.

This very trust, indeed, was the supreme victory of the prophetic faith. Elisha, even with eyes blinded by agony at the thought of what men must suffer in the world-catastrophe Hazael would set in motion, saw spiritual health behind this terrible material surgery. So awful was the calamity when it came that abject terror shrouded the heavens as well as the earth, till men sought to appease the insatiable cruelty of the gods by burning in sacrifice their own

children in the fire. But amid this appalling reign
of desolating fear, the prophets never departed from
the confidence that even the brutal Assyrian, wading
in blood and turning the fruitful earth into a waste,
was only the axe in the hand of the Lord to
destroy that He might build to better purpose,
and to be itself destroyed in the process; or, still
better, the senseless, perishable threshing-instrument
to purge the grain, with no more than the due
proportion of violence, for the sowing of a better
harvest.

As we think of the miseries which the insensate
cruelty of ambitious men has brought upon the world,
we cannot find the prophets' faith an easy victory.
Nor can it be maintained in us except by a deep
sense both of the wickedness and the worth of man's
soul and of the difficulty and blessedness of the
Kingdom which is to be entered by such tribulation.
Only on that estimate can goodness be set above
happiness, and righteousness above quietness, and
the wisdom of God, which uses even cruelty to turn
men to His way of love, be approved.

Finally, we see *utter unscrupulousness*. When the
prophet told him that Benhadad, the king, would
recover from his sickness, yet would not live, Hazael
knew that his murderous secret was out, and, for
the moment, almost seemed to blush. Yet, like
Macbeth, he was not content to say,

If chance will have me king, why, chance can crown me,
Without my stir,

but resolved 'to catch the nearest way,' and be great, 'no matter what illness should attend it.' Benhadad was with him also 'in double trust,' a sovereign who had given him every honour possible for a subject, and a sick man confiding in him as a friend,

> Who should against the murderer shut the door,
> Not bear the knife myself.

But, as his master slept—perhaps the first restful sleep of returning health—Hazael dipped a cloth in water and spread it on his face, careless of the crime that stained his soul and careful only to leave no traces that might mar its success. Then Hazael too might have heard the cry,

> Sleep no more,
> [Hazael] does murder sleep, the innocent sleep,
> Sleep that knits up the ravelled sleave of care,
> The death of each day's life, sore labour's bath,
> Balm of hurt minds, great nature's second course,
> Chief nourisher in life's feast.

Nothing is farther from the mind of God, nothing more utterly 'jumps the life to come,' nothing is more inconceivable as an instrument of God. Yet, how hopeless should we be of any rule of God, had He no way of turning to use the unscrupulous crimes, the perpetrators of which have so often filled earth's highest seats. And when we think of it, what has better shown that 'God too is wise' than the way He diverts astute unscrupulousness to ends quite away from what it purposed.

Only because of this power to use the wickedness

of man for issues the opposite of man's intent, can He at once intrust man with responsibility and rule the world. And because His rule of truth and love never could be achieved, were that responsibility recalled, the instrument is often for terrible rebuke and scourging for all man's sinful state and utter disaster and ruin for itself. The result is not an easy and prosperous and peaceful earth, but the question will not be, whether man has been happy in his course, but whether, finally, God has accomplished His spiritual purpose with him of making him, of his own insight and devotion, a son of God without rebuke in God's Kingdom of truth and righteousness.

2. LET US LOOK AT GOD'S AGENT

Nothing shows the impression a man makes on the popular imagination like the wonderful stories which gather round his name. By that measure, no prophet, not even Elijah, compares with Elisha. And this is the more remarkable that the impression was not made by anything striking in his dress or appearance, as with Elijah. In this very absence of singularity he was a new type of prophet, somewhat as Jesus differed from John the Baptist. The children mocked him, not because he was bald, but because his hair was cut. They were wont to see shaggy men of the wilds like Elijah, and here was an ordinary smooth, trimmed citizen: and no doubt the children reflected the opinion of their seniors that he was a feeble, innocuous imitation of the real article. That was the first impression of the common people, but when they had time to look from the clothes to the man, they understood his significance even better than Hazael, and the mockery of him seemed an appalling piece of impious temerity, to which the tale about the bears, for the warning of impudent little boys in Israel, gives graphic expression.

But Elijah alone understood his full significance. When he called Elisha by casting his mantle over him, he was so overcome by horror at the consequences, that he sought to put off the evil day by undoing his own act, saying, 'Go back; for what have I done to thee?' Elijah knew of Hazael and he knew of Jehu, and his thoughts of both were full of heavy foreboding, but neither of them in all their panoply of war shook his heart with dread like this prosperous yeoman, peacefully superintending his plowmen and himself ploughing among them in his working clothes. In him Elijah saw the forerunner of a new type of prophet by whom God was to hew Israel, whose prophecy, for all its quiet reasonableness, was as dreadful as the lion's roar in the forest or the alarm of the trumpet in the besieged city.

This description of his own work was used by Amos, Elisha's immediate successor, though all his days he remained to outward appearance a simple farmer and shepherd, who never looked or acted the professional prophet or belonged to any prophetic guild. Hosea lived an ordinary married life among his people; Isaiah was a townsman and probably an aristocrat; Jeremiah was a priest, as unlike as possible to a dervish or a revolutionary. From among the people they spoke to people and rulers, and mostly about the human relations they themselves shared with others. Their speech was not passionate or excited, but calmly appealed to reason and conscience. They made large use of writing, the most intellectual invention of civilisation, and they frequently gave what they said studied poetic form.

To the superficial, hasty mind which judges by appearance, they looked plain civilians, more troublesome than important. But to the seeing eye, these agents of God, humbly consecrated to His purpose, with no appeal save to reason and righteousness, and no force except the nature of moral reality and the necessary disaster of selfishness and idolatry, were the most terrible of all judgments on a corrupt civilisation.

God's agent is distinguished from God's mere instrument also by three characteristic marks.

First, he has a quite different estimate from worldly ambition of *what it is worth a man's whole effort to achieve*.

None dreamt of buying Elijah, but, from the lavish presents offered him, Elisha apparently gave the impression of a prosperous man who would naturally accept larger prosperity, could one make it worth his while. But no judgment by appearances was ever more mistaken. His own not inconsiderable possessions he had given up at God's call, and the thought of replacing them by gifts from others never entered his mind. The imposing train of laden camels, which might to another man of his estate have proved as strong a temptation as the kingdom to Hazael, stirred in him no pulse of desire. For Elisha even the glory of an empire was a mere bauble when the morn was breaking blood-red on a doomed world. With that vision of judgment and of high, eternal issues rising out of judgment, whether he ate dry bread or fared sumptuously every day, or went in beggar's rags or royal purple mattered little: and to spend his strength for display or tinsel renown seemed a frivolous use of life and a missing of the values of eternity.

That absorption in higher interests, which, without any ascetic sense of surrender, but by the sheer claims of life's calls, diverts from all mere love of possession and applause, marks all God's true agents.

Second, God's agent carries out his commission *with the Divine compassion in his heart*, announcing no evil he does not share. Hazael exulting and Elisha weeping at the same prospect goes to the heart of the difference between God's mere instrument and His true agent. Every genuine prophet has shared in Elisha's agony. No Old Testament prophet announces the day of calamity without a choking of tears that pleads for a repentance which might avert it. Greatest of all is our Lord weeping over Jerusalem for the disaster even His ministry had failed to avert.

Nor did any of them doubt that they were God's agents in this very thing, that the compassion in their hearts was in His heart also, and that He too would gather His children, as a hen gathers her chickens under her wing, to shield them from every storm, if only they would.

Third, God's agent has *a scrupulous regard for the direct way.*

Here might seem a place only for policy, a call above all to avoid dangerous suggestion. But the direct road to ruin was the one thing God had showed Elisha, and there was for him no other. Beyond it he saw the new world God would rebuild through his suffering servants, and if the way towards it lay through the blotting out of a corrupt civilisation, it was not for him to choose an easier, or, with however heavy a heart, fail to carry out his appointed task in it.

This stirring up of movements fraught with awful judgment for his age may seem a strange task for the passionate lover of his people, but every true agent of God has been engaged in it. The moment he sees that his people's real good is righteousness, not ease, and its worst danger undisturbed corruption; he comes, like the Master, not bringing peace, but a sword, and, like the Apostles, turning the world upside down.

Man's stormy career throughout the ages has been due, above all else, to the ferment of spirit God's agents have stirred up within him, without which he would have grazed peacefully in the best pasture he could find, like other tame animals, or been at times, alone or in small groups, a not very effective beast of prey. Great movements even of destruction demand great loyalties which disregard ease and life itself, all of which prophetic souls have planted. Every true and great and just idea, moreover, is revolutionary amid dead faiths, formal worships, timid submission, material trusts, accepted wrongs. Not by human intent, but by the nature of things, it is disturbing, as the sun, by mere shining in the heavens, gathers the mist into torrent rain, rends the sky with lightning, and turns dead things into putrid corruption. And their justification is the same—the purifying of the air and the cleansing of the earth.

The present unparalleled destruction has been traced back to a simple monk, the son of a charcoal-burner, standing before the mighty of the World and the Church, saying, 'Here I stand. I can do no other, so God help me.' At all events that caused the appalling miseries of the Thirty Years' War; and likely enough they are right who think its desolating effect not yet exhausted. But supposing Luther could have seen all these tremendous consequences of his action, are they right who think he ought to have done something other than God had showed him, and that it would have been better to have left the peoples in quiet serfdom, undisturbed by ideas of liberty, and the Church in undivided superstition, undisturbed by the demand for truth and moral reality?

When we search far enough back for the cause of our calamity, do we not arrive at Jesus Christ Himself? Nothing amazes us more than that this blotting-out of peoples should be the work of Christian nations. But are there any other nations for which it were possible? True it is because they are not really Christian, that the use they make of Christianity is often only the use festering corruption makes of the sun. But our material idolatries might have given us self-interest enough to shun war, had it been crossed by no higher regards; and our corrupt civilisation might have held together longer, had there been in it no energy of higher aspiration. The rulers would not think of sacrificing their sheep as they do their fellows, and the reason is their fear of the Titanic spiritual forces in the souls of men. Nor, without the ideas and devotions, the aspirations and loyalties and consecrations which Christianity has inspired, would they have found the material for such a world-conflagration.

War, moreover, is only a part, the smaller part, of the trouble caused in the world by God's agent. The unrest he has planted in man's soul maintains a perpetual striving and conflict and dissatisfaction which deny mankind under any conditions a placid

Elysium of well-fed ease. So far as it is not mere anxiety and greed, but aspiration and endeavour, this unrest is the measure of man's spiritual progress, even though it be also a gift of sorrow and distress.

For many, religion is purely conservation and comfort, the cement of the present social order, the bulwark of things accepted, the assurance of a prosperous voyage through life and an abundant entrance into the life to come. But even formal religion may only be a sleeping volcano; and a living religion is always a portent in the earth, precisely because, without astute evasions, it must go the way that God has showed it.

God's agent knows that God alone sees the end from the beginning, that unscrupulous policies to direct the issue of events to one's own liking and away from God's are as childish as they are impious, that there is no safe way in which short-sighted mortals cannot err except the plain path of duty, and that there is only one hazard worth taking, the hazard of doing what God demands.

History is a long enough record to show the folly of crooked human policies and the wisdom of simple loyalty to truth and right. The story of Hazael and Elisha does not stand alone, but it is a great example. Before Hazael's unscrupulous astuteness lay a little day of brief authority, and then destruction for the dynasty he had sinned to establish and desolation for the country whose greatness was to maintain his renown. The irony of it all appears in this, that only from the writings inspired by the work of Elisha do later generations know anything of his little honourable career. Before Elisha lay the great and still inspiring teaching of the prophets, the purification of the Exile, and the heaven-scaling spiritual hopes of the Return, and above all Jesus and the Christian Church. And the end is not yet, nor will be till all the work of time is measured by eternity.

The greatest of us who seeks, by his own devices and in disregard for others, to achieve his own personal ambitions, will only make a little noise for a little time in our little world, then pass into oblivion with all his work turned to other ends than his own. But the least of us who lives only for God's purposes, guided alone by what God has showed, will, in our own degree, add to God's eternal treasure of good, and not ourselves pass away from our share in the inheritance, but be heirs of God and joint-heirs with Jesus Christ.

All wickedness makes God's way with men necessarily harder, and the realisation of His Kingdom necessarily through greater agony both for Himself and His children. Yet, even by it, God is not mocked in His government of the world, nor hindered in achieving its end. But for man, drawing his little breath on earth between the eternities, the one serious task, a task that has all the powers of the universe on its side, is to know the will of God in humility and to do it in simple obedience and full purpose of heart. Then only can we know that, measured both by time and eternity, our labour is not in vain in the Lord.

> Let no mortal leave
> The onward path, although the earth should gape
> And from the gulf of hell 'Destruction' cry,
> To take dissimulation's winding way.

IV

REBUILDING

Isaiah ix. 9–10. 'And all the people shall know, even Ephraim and the inhabitant of Samaria, that say in pride and in stoutness of heart, The bricks are fallen, but we will build with hewn stone: the sycomores are cut down, but we will change them into cedars.'

THE exact time when these words were first spoken and the precise situation to which they originally applied are uncertain, but the place they now occupy in the book of Isaiah shows that the temper of which they speak was thought to be characteristic of Israel up to the first Assyrian invasion.

Throughout the long reign of Jeroboam II the Northern Kingdom had enjoyed unexampled prosperity. She seemed peculiarly secure, not only in her own strength, but in an alliance with Syria, her nearest and most powerful neighbour and hitherto her chief adversary.

The preceding passage about Zebulun and the land of Naphtali tells of a new and greater danger. Beyond Syria to the north-east lay Assyria. A common soldier called Pul had there risen to the top in days of revolution. With the usual conqueror's appropriation of the Deity, he expanded his name to Tiglath-pil-eser, which means the god Tiglath helps Pul. He proved something of a Napoleon, and, under his leadership, Assyria took one of those military fevers which seem to make men and even women dream of nothing save war and conquest. On any pretext or none she fell on her neighbours, and, as Isaiah expresses it, gathered the nations as one gathers eggs. For the securing of the empire thus won military measures were resorted to, of which the Turk, at his worst, is the only modern parallel. Transportation of whole peoples, extensive planting among them of aliens, tribute, wholesale robbery, rape, murder and slavery so terrorised the suffering peoples that even their religion became a ghastly fear of gods who could only be appeased by human sacrifice. And then the Assyrian, after thus turning the garden into a wilderness, boasted of it as the extension of civilisation.

In face of such an experience, was it not true pride and real stoutness of heart in Israel to be able to say, 'The bricks have fallen, but we will build with hewn stone'? Is there not here an unconquerable buoyancy and native courage we must admire; and have we not a right to expect victory over any calamity for so tough and virile a people?

Moreover, there was an element of faith in it as well as of pertinacity. The mass of the religious teachers said, We are God's chosen people; ours is a purer religion and a higher civilisation; we were at peace, and our alliances were for defence and not for aggression; we were rich, but by peaceful commerce. As God is on our side, we cannot forever be overborne by an unholy spirit of domination. And, though they were more concerned to say what was acceptable than what was true, they were not wholly mistaken.

Yet there were a few men, scarcely more than one or two in a generation, men as unpopular as they were few, who spoke to a quite different purpose. While others were still living in undisturbed security, they had already announced the calamity; and now they continued to say, You will never rebuild the old edifice with any material.

This attitude was the more amazing that they alone of all men were undismayed by the might of the foe. For them Assyria was a mere senseless axe in the hand of a Higher Power, doomed herself also presently to destruction. She might fill the world with clamour and boast herself against any God who was not her own private possession, but the issue of impious brutality, these prophets knew, was self-destruction. To-day she speaks only in arrogant inscriptions, made permanent by being engraved on stone, and in writings, mostly about material possessions, still extant because burned into brick; but there is no vital word in them for any living soul, and they are commentated by the barren mounds, once great cities, from which they are dug. This the prophets foresaw, not, as it has been the fashion lately to maintain, by political foresight, but by religious insight into the principles upon which God determines the destinies of men and nations.

Alone they stood in that age, free from fear of man, emancipated by faith in a God who never comes short in power or wisdom or purpose of good, a God whose judgment even is in mercy. Yet they never wavered in their quite hopeless outlook on the material situation; and they continued to say to their contemporaries, Not only is your self-confidence vain, but also your religious trust is the pride which goes before a deeper fall and the stoutness of heart which persists to the final disaster. Such a message naturally seemed to those who heard it both unpatriotic and irreligious, but, unfortunately for Israel, it proved to be true.

The basis of this judgment was quite simple. The bricks, the prophets said, fell from the weakness of the building, and not from the violence of the assault. With different spiritual conditions conquest might never have happened; and, in any case, nations do not crumble before mere conquest. The cause which made the disaster so utter was the turning of the nation's moral cement into sand. And it was irretrievable, because no amendment of men's individual ways was providing better mortar.

The meaning of the prophets is plain enough in what they say of men, but the peculiar quality of their judgment comes out even more definitely in what they say of women. Nothing marks so clearly their estimate of what is important and unimportant, strong and weak, than the peculiar value assigned to woman's influence.

John Knox, when asked how he could be so bold with Queen Mary, replied, "I have looked in the face of many angry men and not been overly afeard: why should I fear the pleasing face of a gentle-woman?" But the prophets argued otherwise. Their whole judgment of life depended on looking in the face of the Assyrian trooper and not being at all afraid, and being filled with foreboding when they looked in the face of the Israelite gentlewoman.

A recent writer has proclaimed the attainment by the fairer half of humanity of power as the advent of something like the millennium. But, even in that remote age and in that oriental society, the prophets seem to have thought that woman had already arrived very mightily at power. The quantity of her influence they seem to have thought practically unlimited, but being apparently of Mrs Poyser's opinion that 'God made the women to match the men,' they were less sure of the quality, taking the question of the use of power to be of character and not of sex.

We shall not understand in the least what they say unless we realise first the reverence that was in them for true womanhood. The sternest of all is Amos who speaks of the gentlewomen of Samaria as 'kine of Bashan' who crush the needy and say unto their lords, 'Bring and let us drink.' Yet he speaks sorrowfully of Israel as a virgin; and the saddest thing he knows is the fair virgin going into captivity. Hosea still more definitely regards the corruption of the women as the root of the national disintegration, but he repudiates the idea of one morality for the man and another for the woman, and his own unquenchable love for his erring wife was the well-spring of his unfaltering faith in a God who would never lose His tenderness for His erring people. Isaiah calls his wife the prophetess, as if she freely and equally shared both the burden and the hope of his high calling, while Ezekiel's wife is described as the light of his eyes. No crime is greater to Micah than casting out the women of his people from their pleasant homes; and he cannot think of any figure for frustrated endeavour like the anguish of travail without the joy of motherhood.

If we bear that sympathy and reverence in mind, we shall understand what Isaiah meant by his elaborate assault upon the finery which was carried with mincing steps and wanton eyes along the streets of his native city. What hurt him was the idea that woman was a mere peg to hang clothes on for man's gratification, and that one to whom God had given tenderness and helpfulness should be so blind and callous as to take advantage of the riches which war brings to the few, amid the abject misery which it works for the many. Every detail of the offensive display burnt itself into his soul, because it seemed to him the final mark of the thoughtless selfishness which is the dissolution of society, the final denial of any hope of permanent recovery, the thing which said most loudly that, for all his people's suffering,

God's anger was not turned away, but His hand was stretched out still.

Finally, as the end drew near, Jeremiah saw its most ominous threat in a king who would place his womenfolk in a palace ceiled with cedar and painted with vermilion, at the cost of the oppression, the poverty, the miseries of the common people.

But the callous luxury of the women did not concern the women alone. It was the mark of false values in men and women alike, showing that the men also had lost faith in the divine things of purity and tenderness and the beauty of holiness and inward peace. In both alike it proved the loss of the justice and trust between man and man which alone can preserve any social structure from becoming a heap of ruins.

Compared with this decay of the spiritual mortar, the assault of the Assyrian was a trivial incident. Israel might still be a highly religious nation in all that concerned creed and ceremonial, but God was not in all her people's ways; and, for the prophets, God and His requirements and purposes were the only realities in the world which might not, without disaster, be disregarded. And, so far as Israel at least was concerned, they were not mistaken.

This is very ancient history, but it is the nature of history to be constantly repeating itself. And a story of long ago has the advantage over our present experience that it has been told to the end and its prophetic principles have been tested by the final issue. Wherefore, it may still shed some light for us upon what is truly strong and what is weak, upon what will sustain our society and what will expose it to dissolution, upon what we purpose in faith and what we purpose in mere pride and stoutness of heart.

In the middle of the War a minister of state prophesied to us, saying: "This country, therefore, so far from being impoverished, will be richer in everything that constitutes real and true wealth. We shall be a better organised, better equipped, better trained, and, what is more important perhaps, a better disciplined nation." The context made plain that a greater edifice of material wealth was meant and that it was to be built by more elaborate organisation, and that the cement of it, which is called discipline, was really drill. Apparently we are to have more capital than ever, and the masses are to be still more pliant to its control, and mechanical production is to be more than ever man's chief occupation. We shall sit in a more unassailable security, our hands gathering the treasure of the whole earth; and, if the smoke of our chimneys, as we work it up for a world which war has sent back to the shovel and the plough, is a denser curtain than ever between us and the sun, we shall have compensation when, in the reign of a new Solomon, the silver is as stones. And if wealth, as of old, increases the slum, how will it glorify the palace! 'The bricks are fallen but we will build

with hewn stone; the sycomores are cut down, but
we will change them into cedars.' And the Peace
seems to have been made to prophesy in the same
vein even more than the War.

The vast sacrifice of life for those who are gone
and of happiness for those they have left behind
are to secure for any who are alive and have heart
to begin again the old order in greater splendour,
with the old scurry and rivalry, the old driving
of the weak to the wall, the old round of trivial
distractions, the old care for what we shall eat and
what we shall drink and wherewithal we shall be
clothed, the old marrying and giving in marriage
for every reason except love and mutual esteem, the
old measuring of worth by possession, the old
materialism and externality which has made us
barren for so long in every field of original production, and which has made religion a mere buttress of
respectability. And many are content to have it so.

But possibly God meaneth not so: and, though
we have not thought much about His methods and
purposes, they may, after all, be of consequence in
the final issue. Perhaps the bricks have fallen more
than we yet realise. Capital which has become
debt is merely exaction without equivalent. At no
time was its distribution determined by the value
of service rendered, but, taken as a whole, capital
formerly had behind it somewhere the benefits of
past labours. But when it has been blown into the
air and exists nowhere, how long will its nominal

recognition continue to be of value? In any case, sooner or later, the old system is going to fall. Will the bricks of individual competition be replaceable by the hewn stone of organisation, whether of socialism or, as it rather appears at present, of monopolistic trusts?

But what if the issue does not really concern either, and if, as of old, the real problem of security is neither brick nor stone, but mortar? And what if that must be ethical and spiritual? What if drill as a substitute is mere dividing sand? What if our real strength and greatness depend more on how we spend than on what we get, on our homes than on our workshops, on the thoughts of our women than on the swords of our warriors?

The old order may not pass without causing much suffering we rightly fear and the loss of many blessings we rightly cherish. A poorer, narrower, obscurer age may ensue. But if we can exchange pride and self-indulgence and lust of dominion and callous rivalry and vain activities and measureless discontent for peace of heart and brotherly relations and the simple and beautiful arts of living, we shall be well repaid both for our suffering and for our loss.

Primarily it is a question of what are life's best possessions. That is determined for us by the things unseen and eternal, which are according to man's soul and not his circumstances or visible belongings. Being thus simply human, they are not different for any of us, rich or poor, learned or ignorant, man or woman. For the most part, though so lofty in principle, they come down in practice to the plain issue of being ready in daily life to deny ourselves all good not justly and mercifully won, to seek, in contentment·with such things as we have, the beauty of inward peace, to set above luxuries the purity of our homes and the sacredness of our affections: in short to value life itself above all its trappings.

In Christ, in this sense, there is neither male nor female. We must all alike be concerned to discover that love alone is mighty to bind men together in a more excellent fellowship, and that the things of love concern our moral valuation of persons and not our material valuation of things. And we shall need to devote ourselves to its service with high courage and devotion, if we are not to return to a primitive barbarism in which men fight and women toil.

But, while we are alike in the duty of consecrating all our gifts, we are not alike in the measure of the gifts we have to consecrate. Perhaps, therefore, I may be pardoned if I ask you women, and more particularly you younger women, with your greater endowment for the personal aspect of life, to weigh your enormous influence for good and evil.

When real, woman is more sincere than man; when sympathetic, more wisely helpful; when devoted, more courageous; when spiritual, more direct in arriving at the central issues. But we all have the defects of our qualities, when we fail to realise them. Wherefore, when woman is blind, she can more effectively shut her eyes, when ambitious be more unscrupulous, when material make greater sacrifices of truer blessings for display. In your hands largely is the question of a simpler, quieter, more human and contented life. What is needed above all else is the recovery of your great gift for discerning character, and for teaching that nothing in all the world makes up for true comradeship in the battle of life. Is there any cause of the chaos in our social life so certain or so powerful as the dazzling of this insight by the glitter of wealth and foolish social fallacies?

In the end the matter is for all of us a question, not of resolve, but of faith. Unless we believe in God as the final might and the things of God, which are justice and sympathy and the spirit of peace and the service of love, as the final good, we shall none of us ever build to wiser, kinder, more spiritual, and, therefore, lasting purpose, than in former days; and the higher the edifice, either of brick or hewn stone, the intenser our effort and the vaster our organisation, the more certain it is to fall in ever more hopeless ruin.

V

GOD'S IDEAL AND MAN'S REALITY

ISAIAH ii. 5. 'O house of Jacob, come ye, and let us walk in the light of the Lord.'

MUCH of the prophetic literature was collected, not by the prophets themselves, but by their disciples, and that amid a ruin and chaos which admitted of little opportunity for studying chronology or order. Our text might, therefore, be a mere isolated ejaculation remembered only because of its impressive form, to which we could attach no precise meaning, because we no longer know in what connection it was originally spoken. But if the connection in which it now stands affords a clear meaning, there can be no good reason for doubting that we have the original setting in which its author himself put it.

Our text is preceded by the great poem which is still the most memorable of all songs of peace; and it is followed by a prose description of a country where everything is the absolute opposite of this hope. Are we to suppose that this intense contrast both in form and matter is a mere happy accident of juxtaposition, without any intention on the part either of the author or his editor? And this is the less probable that, when we read the passage as one whole, with our text as the connecting link, it takes on a clear and vivid meaning, and the impression both of the poem of ideal peace and the prose of actual calamity is intensified.

The light of the Lord in which men are called to walk is, in that case, nothing other than the ideal of perfect peace in perfect righteousness of which the prophet has just sung, and the House of Jacob he summons to walk in it is just the idolatrous material people whose debasement and calamity he goes on to describe. Then the whole passage is the great appeal of religion to walk by faith in God's eternal purpose and not by sight of man's present securities, to walk amid the world's idolatries as those who know that the Lord God omnipotent alone reigns.

The saying may still appear an abrupt ejaculation, but it is the abruptness of a shining stream between a mountain and a morass, which at once marks their connection and heightens their contrast.

It summons us dwellers on the low morasses where the malaria breeds to lift up our eyes to the mountain of God's unchanging purpose, which soars serene above all the hills of human endeavour, from whence alone comes the pure air to fill our lungs with health and give us strength to keep pressing forward towards those heavenly steeps.

If you climb the western slope of the Jura and suddenly come out at the top upon the panorama of the Alps, your first impression is of the whole

earth tilted up into the sky, until you discover that
what seemed a rampart of cloud is the real range
of the snow mountains. Then all the vast masses
of the Oberland seem to sink to a lower plane, and
rather to lie below you than to tower above.

The ideal of the Lord shines high and distant on
our horizon like that solemn silver range, and the
question which decides all the levels of human endeavour is whether it is solid mountain or mere cloud
phantasy.

Through countless centuries this hope has stood
there in its dim impressiveness, seemingly little nearer
for all man's longing and endeavour. Some two thousand six hundred years have passed since Isaiah made
this appeal; and, as the poem is found only slightly
different in his contemporary Micah and is not like
the style of either, probably it is a quotation and still
older. That it was old and familiar may even be the
point of Isaiah's appeal. Here, he would say, is the
long dreamed of, long accepted ideal of the Lord
which you all know: and here still, in sad contrast,
is the actual House of Jacob, in no dimmest fashion
changed into the likeness of it.

Eight centuries after Isaiah, the prophecy of the
New Testament ends as the prophecy of the Old
began. The author of the Book of Revelation pre-
dicts a new Jerusalem which is still essentially the
old ideal of perfect peace in perfect righteousness.
But he is still waiting for it to come down from
God out of heaven, while the actual world he lived

in was as full as ever of idolatry, which had still in
its train the devastating harvest of lies and murders
and impending disasters.

Since then nearly two millenniums have passed,
and is this new Jerusalem much nearer being built,
either in 'England's green and pleasant land,' or
in any other country beneath the sun? The weight
of armaments even in peace oppressed the nations.
Suspicion and dread shadowed the intercourse of
the peoples, and all the acquired dexterities of
centuries were devoted to the arts of war. And now,
never from Isaiah's own day, when the Assyrian
was gathering the nations like eggs, and glorying
in making men slaves and turning large portions of
the earth into a desert, has there been a direr contrast to his ideal of peace. Scarce a nation remains
which has not lifted up its sword against another;
the ploughshare itself has become only another kind
of sword; the first law which goes forth from any
Zion is the might of the strongest; and the final
word of destiny is taken to be poison gas and
torpedoes. But why are we astray on this perilous
path? Is it the failure of God's light or man's
failure to walk in it?

We had, indeed, long been told that it was time
men gave up all notions of Divine ideals, all dreams
of walking in any light but man's, and contented
themselves with working for such immediate earthly
good as they might reasonably hope to see attained.
Instead of dreaming of a perfect reign of God, we

were to set ourselves to work for as perfect a reign
of man as may be, having learned that all beyond
sprang from the uncritical phantasy of the childhood
of the race. Having suffered the disenchantment of
knowledge, we were, as practical people, to dismiss
the whole business of religion as a distraction from
life's effective task of realising time's nearer hopes.
Instead of childishly wasting our time building
castles in the air, we were to provide adequate
cottages upon earth, and accomplish this and other
material reforms, not by appeals to righteousness,
but by getting to work at once with the organisation
of science and the strong hand of legislation.
Personal appeals to the heart and conscience, we
were assured, had only been shackles on progress
and the true reason why it 'halted on palsied feet.'
We were, therefore, to drill and march men in
companies into a golden age to be created by
compulsory education and a universally organised
abundance.

For many long years of prosperity these material
and immediate schemes for improving the world
seemed full of promise; and their acceptance was
thought to mark the advent of the true millennium,
from which we might new date the progress of the
world.

Yet this very trust in gain and not in godliness,
in means and not in men was the very state of
things from which the prophets augured an era of
disaster; and a man is a prophet as he is not dazzled

by present prosperity, but reads from the hearts of men the issues of life.

With all its promise, the business languished: and the very thing it lacked was just the vitalising breath of reverence for God's image in His children.

Education did a great work, yet somehow it did not educate, its most immediate result being to expose millions of undisciplined minds in all classes to a flood of distracting nonsense and misleading suggestion.

Again our mastery over nature and our organisation of industry were stupendous achievements, but they failed to serve our real human needs. Its most obvious result was to turn men into machines, pack them in dense city areas, and expose them to continual uncertainty of employment.

Our national enterprise achieved the vastest empire. But the good it accomplished had its reverse side of selfish policies, which, in exploiting the weak, exposed the austerity of our toil and the equality of our justice to dangers no conquering people has wholly escaped.

Riches won by selfish dexterity and concentration on material interests were spent with a wastefulness and pride of display which made all the bitterer the vast poverty which they increased and did not remove. Our state was coming to be a worse denial of the eternal righteousness and the things of the soul than even the brutalities and horrors of war, just because it was so calmly accepted as the necessary and even blessed order of the world.

It was the old story of the House of Jacob, of a land full of silver and gold, and of abject, grinding poverty; a land full of chariots and horses, and of ruthless competition and the unchecked might of the strong. And the heart of the evil was the same— a land full of idols, a land of mean material reverences and the covetousness which is the blind selfish essence of idolatry. This worldliness is the miasma of life's low levels, and the nation which breathes it only cannot, by any organisation, effort or material success, ever be in health and vigour.

Even the Church, our special spiritual House of Jacob, whose very business it is to live by the ideal of God's righteous rule and finished purpose, languished in this atmosphere, being also replenished from the East, having her own devices of display, her own forms of worldliness, her own material trusts, her own worship of visible power, her own undivine venerations, and, in consequence, her own bitterness and suspicions and strifes about things unworthy and unessential.

To shut our eyes to our real state is calamitous illusion; and nothing stands so much between us and a triumphant vision of faith. No true word of God ever blinks a fact, and no one is a prophet except as he sees deeper into evil and feels more bitterly oppression and wrong than other men. The most notable figures in human history are the heroic, lonely prophetic souls who, in days of prosperity, have looked through all shams and unrealities and gone straight to the thoughts and faiths of men. They alone proved themselves able to meet the days of supreme conflict which they had foreseen, with unfaltering courage, because they had also the vision of the rule and purpose of God.

Can they, with their penetrating and far-seeing eyes, have been wrong in thinking this rule and purpose the only abiding reality, while we, with our purblind and earthly vision, are right in regarding all higher hopes as mere cloud phantasm?

What surer proof can we have that their vision of hope was no illusion than the certainty that their interpretation of life was no mistake? While our senses are dulled by repetition, till we unthinkingly accept iniquity, because, amazing reason! it is common, they were delivered from the blindness of custom, and found the persistence of wrong no palliation, but, as it is in reality, its worst horror, and saw every crime as freshly as when the startled earth first drank the blood of Abel, as new for him who commits it and for him who suffers from it.

Because of this same fresh and inspired insight, they not only foresaw war, but they understood all its calamity, never losing the individual in the mass or thinking in terms of armies and political changes. They felt war, as it truly is, as the individual agonies of human terror when all men prided themselves on was laid low and the idols they trusted in proved vain and they sheltered in holes and caves like the wild creatures. Yet it was precisely in this storm,

when it came, that the prophetic hope of a Day of
the Lord, which was to transform all this desolation
into perfect peace in perfect holiness, blazed up to
its full splendour.

This great hymn of God's rule and the end of war
came out of no time of piping peace. If we listen
aright, we hear in it the sob of a people robbed
and spoiled. The need of the country was plough-
shares, for

> All her husbandry doth lie on heaps
> Corrupting in its own fertility;

and pruning hooks, for all her hedges are

> Like prisoners wildly o'ergrown with hair;

and law, for 'the tabernacles of robbers prosper,'
and 'the poor of the earth hide themselves like wild
asses in the desert'; and a Word of the Lord, for
the whole higher nature decays when men

> nothing do but meditate on blood.

Yet the essence of the prophetic view is that it
is vain to begin with war, vain to think we can guard
against it by any reorganisation of force; and they
would have had just as little hope in a League of
Nations by itself as in any other device of human
policy. You cannot have peace till you first have
justice, and justice first between individuals, and
not first between nations. While you have the
'glooming alleys' on the one hand, and, on the
other, a 'wide house built by unrighteousness and
its spacious chambers ceiled with cedar and painted

vermilion by injustice,' you have a state of things more calamitous for all that God seeks in His children than even the desolation of war. And you cannot have justice till you have first rid your souls of idolatry, for the covetous soul is essentially and radically unjust. Therefore, the last question about society is, What do men reverence, what do they adore and trust? So long as they worship position not balanced by responsibility, military power indifferent to justice, wealth careless of humanity, they cannot have peace. What one man has only as another wants necessarily breeds strife; and what rests on force logically justifies the strong in taking what they think they require. Not till we worship God by reverence for man made in His image, and believe that the final might in the world is truth and character and service and the spirit of love, can war be a struggle for peace or anything more than a blotting out of humanity for material policies. Nor can we ever hope to bring the forces into operation which will make an end of war while we worship the things for which wars are made. War may be the fever, but idolatry is the malaria, and the fever is recuperative only as we get rid of the malaria. And this we can do only as we draw our breath from the mountain of the Lord and not from the miasma of our own low material reverences.

Hence the great ideal hopes of the prophets came out of ages when the actual state of society led other men to despair. The reason was not merely that men long most ardently for what they least possess, but that, when the idols which block up the temples of our hearts are broken, we may see the high altar of the patient goodness of God; when the chambers of our imagery, in which we sit in the narrow circle of our dim human candles, are unroofed, we may come out into the light of the Lord. That light shines of itself and we have no need to paint it 'costly gay,' but we cannot walk in it so long as we are walled in by the illusions of our idolatries, and accept the unrighteousness by which we profit as the eternal order of the world, and seek to live in a private heaven for ourselves of isolated opulence.

Most confidently, therefore, in times when man's trust in man 'whose breath is in his nostrils and is nothing to be accounted of' was broken, the prophet looked for a Day of the Lord when God's patient working would have won the hearts of His children and perfect peace would be established in perfect righteousness: and then most earnestly he called upon men to walk in the light of it. He was like the physician who, just because he has traced disease to one prolific form of life, in the day of pestilence sees it carried on every breath of polluted air, yet finds security in windows open towards heaven, and never ceases to dream that, just because he has traced the infection to one root, it may be utterly extirpated. Thus the prophet's more terrible diagnosis of our disease, which finds it no rash of the skin to be healed with salves, but a malady of the heart which 'is deceitful above all things and desperately wicked,' is also the ground of his hope, for he is no longer concerned with reforms which heal one sore only to see another break out, but with a single radical conversion from worship of the things seen and temporal to trusting the things unseen and eternal.

Our fellowship is religious as we feel the personal sorrow and desolation of war, yet penetrate beneath it to injustice, and beneath injustice to idolatry, and from that discovery to the hope of a new reverence for the things of God which are in the hearts of His children.

The nation which can make this discovery and say, 'Come and let us walk in the light of the Lord,' will be established in righteousness; against the Church which makes this call its supreme business the gates of hell will not prevail. But, above all, each one who knows for himself has the victory which overcomes the world, even if our House of Jacob —be it country or church—continue in idolatry. The Church of those met in the name of Him over whom the world's idolatries had no power, will not, we may hope, wholly fail us, but if it did and we should have to stand alone, as His Cross means victory over the idolatries of fears, possessions, favours, we can bear our solitary witness, heroic, even tragic, if required of us, in public action or public appeal, if that be our duty, or privately, humbly, by what we are, rather than by what we do or say, if that be the way of God's appointing.

We may still have to live long on the low un-drained fens, and to realise that, in the fulfilment of His purpose, a thousand years are with God as one day, but we shall never question that the mountain of the House of the Lord is established above all the hills of human powers and policies, because it will not only be the shining goal of our aspirations, but its divine air will enable us, as we wait on the Lord in times of great depression, 'to mount up with wings as eagles,' in times of great strain, 'to run and not be weary,' and above all, in the long common day when nothing happens save the monotony of toil and endurance, 'to walk and not faint.' Precisely in the darkness and the storm when earthly lights are blotted out, we have most need to look to heaven and discover that only what is above earth's turmoil can be our guiding light in the midst of its darkness and its distress.

VI

THE LIGHT OF THE WORLD

JOHN xii. 46. 'I am come a light into the world, that whosoever
believeth on me should not abide in darkness.'

THE idea of Jesus as the light of the world has
been made so familiar to you from infancy by word
and picture that probably it has never occurred to
you to ask whether you really believe it. Still less
perhaps have you ever conceived that you might
mistake the meaning of a figure so simple. Yet
many have vehemently and passionately denied that
it is true; and sometimes at least through a misunderstanding which is not confined to unbelievers.

To many 'the pale Galilean' seems to have passed
like the shadow of a black cloud over a formerly
sun-lit world. They say He changed the old full-
blooded pagan joy in living into a timid, anaemic
anxiety about one's soul, and replaced the courageous
and self-respecting morality of free men by a slavish
subjection and cringing humility. Especially they
think that He turned the cult of beauty and grace
and the fullness of a glad existence into the morbid
cult of suffering and death. Moreover, this seems
to them as erroneous as it is gloomy. Did not He
teach meek submissiveness: and does not science
teach success to the successful fighter for his own

hand? Is not even His teaching about love a mistaken sentimentality about the laggards, which retards the race in its progress? Above all His Cross, we are told, so far from being light in the world, is the blackest shadow which has ever fallen upon its brightness. It is no object of contemplation for strong, virile, energetic men, but only for the ascetic, the effeminate, the feeble, the terror-stricken. Thus to no Jew of ancient times was the Cross more of an offence than it was, for example, to Heine: and to many seekers after wisdom, now as formerly, it is foolishness.

We must not shirk this issue, for, till it is decided, there is no believing in Jesus, with such belief, at least, as He intended. If they are right, He was wrong: and, till we see that He was right, real belief in Him there cannot be. To come a light into the world is to show the world as it truly is and its uses as they genuinely profit. If He was only a mistaken enthusiast, the sooner we radically and emphatically disbelieve in Him the better, because the quality of light is to enlighten, and not to shed a mere delusive radiance.

If the Preacher was on the right road when he sought wisdom in the sense of the knowledge which is power, and gave himself to mirth, and withheld nothing from his eyes that they desired, and gained for himself a great estate and a large retinue to minister to his pleasure and his pride, Jesus was, beyond all question, utterly mistaken. To see how utterly mistaken He was we need only to remember what He said about not laying up treasure, not exercising lordship over others, not desiring tokens of respect. It is still more apparent from what He was and what He did, what He suffered others to do to Him, what He thought good and what He thought bad, what He thought low and what He thought high. Above all, we see the difference in what He thought weak and what He thought strong. If aggressive might is really strong and love which suffers long and is kind is weak, He shed no light whatsoever upon the world, but was simply the most mistaken man who ever lived.

Frequently, at least, He is thought wrong merely because His teaching is misunderstood, as though by love He meant a soft emotional way of living which makes us submit to the world's evils and oppressions. Not till we discern that it is a triumphant way of bearing ourselves which gives us victory over them, is it possible to see that He alone of men truly knew the world as God has really made it and manifested the one successful way of using it for the end for which God designed it. Nor till we make that discovery do we, in any right sense, believe that He came a light into it.

Plainly there are two possibilities of mistake. We may be mistaken about the world, or we may be mistaken about Jesus. There is even a third possibility, the most likely of all. We may be mistaken both about the world and about Jesus: and perhaps no one who has ever seriously reflected upon both ever falls back upon a worldly valuation of the world and the self-centred way of conquering it except by this double mistake.

The wrong view depends on what we may call the iridescent idea of light, the idea of it as mere pleasing brightness. Not that in itself even this is wrong. On the contrary, in its right place and with deep enough thoughts to interpret it, it is wholly right and beautiful, and it may even be true and sublime. The artist, for example, does not use light merely to make visible his subject. Perhaps he fills his picture with light, but even then he uses it to set some things in brightness and some things in shade, to refresh your spirit with variety; and somewhere on the horizon he fills a large open space with pure clear radiance to touch you to reverence with the sense of infinity. And in the very deepest way Jesus has come a light into the world after this manner.

No effect of His presence in the world was more speedily apparent than the awakening in the human heart of a new range of emotions stirred by the new splendour shed on the more gracious aspects of human life; and perhaps it is not wrong to ascribe to Him also a new sense of the beauty and meaning even of the world of nature. Above all He calls forth in us a sense of the serenity and peace and measureless depth of the heavens above our troubled earth, like those mysterious infinite depths which, even amid the storm wrack, shine in vast spaces of the far horizon.

Till he has thus ministered to our spirits something of the splendour even of the soiled and troubled earth, and of the serenity even of the storm-rent heavens above it, and especially till He has shed a new glory on the face of every child of man, we have no response in us equal to any judgment of the true beauty of the world or the true dignity of our humanity. The light must be upon the world as it is, but till it touch our own hearts to respond to its appeal, the highest and best in it must remain meaningless or quite unknown.

When we think, as those who deliberately reject Christ have thought, that the abiding good of the world consists in the things of pleasure and possession and the using of others for the service of our desires and our self-exaltation, in the things which the Preacher found to be vanity and vexation of spirit, is it because they are our true good, or only because our souls, never having been touched to finer issues, have never seen life in the true light of the spirit?

Yet even here the corruption of the best is the worst. It is easy to conceive of Christ as a light in the world in the form of mere cheering radiance, altering nothing and revealing nothing, as a mere comfortable way of thinking without any relation to the realities of life. To how many is that gilding of the face of reality the beginning and the end of religion, so that Jesus is to them ever a stained-glass window figure with shining halo, pleasing to turn aside on occasion to contemplate, but in no sense revealing anything which makes the world a new creation!

How much of our religion is merely sentimental, concerned with emotional relaxations, and in no way with the stern business of living! Yet Jesus Himself is never sentimental and He never omitted anything from the scope of His religion or ever regarded it as less than victory over life's actual ills.

While He promised that true belief in Him would enable us all our days and in every kind of duty to walk in light, He never promised that we should always walk in brightness. On the contrary He rather seems to have thought that His light would be of most profit and succour when it rose upon a world shattered and derelict.

The light of Christ is not a mere way of suggesting cheerfulness to ourselves, as when frightened children in the night squeeze their eyes till they produce a kind of ghostly brightness, though they know well that the darkness around is still unaltered. The final purpose of light is just to enable you to see—nothing more and nothing less. It is peace, but only as our fears pass with the darkness, and security, but only as menacing shadow turns to refreshing shade, and victory, but only as we discern all right ways of doing with the dawn. It sums up all we ought to include in salvation, yet only as the wanderer in the waste finds his way home because the sun has lit up the whole landscape till he can guide himself by all its features.

Directly light is not for your consolation and exaltation at all: and it may be far otherwise. When you are trying to save men from a wrecked ship and you wait in agony for the dawn, it is not to give you an artistic sense of a picturesque scene or the emotional satisfaction of a moving spectacle as it displays the seething ocean pouring over cramped figures clinging to broken cordage. You know it will wring your heart with new anguish, but you think nothing of that if it help you to bring the victims ashore. Is it not time that we thought less of our immediate feelings and realised Christ's coming as just such a harrowing light upon a scene of desolation to enable us to help in saving the crew of a shipwrecked world?

Never, in our time at least, have men longed for the dawn, through long winter nights, as they did in the trenches. Those at home often thought of the cold and the wet and the danger, but did they realise how terribly the hardship was increased simply by the horror of thick darkness? And yet the light only displayed the desolation and the danger. But in that very openness men found cheer and peace, and could once more smile and even sleep. And for brave men it will ever be so. They will ever desire above all else to see life as it really is and face the conflict and know their own place in it with a clear discernment of their duty; and they will fear no difficulty or danger if they are assured of not walking in darkness.

When the Church came to observe the season we now call Christmas as the anniversary of the coming of Jesus as a light into the world, it was neither because of any ecclesiastical ruling nor of any tradition, but simply from a sense of the fitness of things. Christmas was just the ancient New Year, the first day of the visibly increasing light; and they meant that His coming was to them the sure promise of the passing of the 'winter of their discontent.'

To realise the feeling which directed this choice, we must not think of our warm well-lit firesides, with our books and busy social intercourse, but of an open-air people, whose houses were mere shelters, cold, imperfectly lit, inadequately weatherproof, in which, except among the very rich, there was little furniture and no books. Thus the winter nights were a long weariness and discomfort. Also we must take account of pagan superstitions about the struggle of the powers of light with the powers of darkness, which the lengthening day yearly proved to be decided in favour of the powers of light.

But, still more, for our purpose, it is important that Jesus was first conceived as coming into the world on the day of the new light and that the custom of observing the day spread during years when the ancient civilisation was going down in appalling chaos and agony. Moreover men still knew what they were talking about when they spoke of the religion of Jesus, because it still stood so clearly over against the ancient paganism that they did not talk of

Jesus when they meant Jupiter, as is only too common in our day. They knew that He meant a certain view of the world, a certain way of meeting its calamities, a certain course of conduct amid its perplexities, a certain kind of valuation of its good and its evil, a certain attitude of forbearance and forgiveness, in short, a certain way of being conquerors over life's ills and antagonisms. They conceived Him to be a light upon all God's strange doings, and a guidance, whereby, in the worst private calamity and public upheaval, they did not walk in darkness.

Not perhaps in the same degree, but in a degree at least which gives every thoughtful person a sense of futility and sometimes of despair, we also are in need of light upon our time and our way in it. And if Christ is not a light in it, who is? Certainly not those who preached the glory of the confident and the triumph of the strong!

The first question concerns what this light truly is. To that there is a quite direct and simple answer. It concerns God's own notions about His own world, and how He rules it, and for what end.

The testing issue is the relation of righteousness and reward.

The history of revelation is, in essence, the history of this question. Even religious men began with the belief that God maintains the righteous in prosperity and only mocks the wicked with temporary illusions of success. In human justice this wrought out as an eye for an eye and a tooth for a tooth.

Only very slowly was it realised that this view was inconsistent with the facts of life and inadequate to our right relations one to another. With this negative conclusion went an increasing positive conviction that God's wisdom wrought with a larger vision, because it was determined by a love to men, not only more patient and more kind, but also more wise, than mere justice. This wrought out in practice in the devoted, self-forgetting labour of God's suffering servant, who bore others' griefs and carried others' sorrows.

But it was left to Jesus to deny, by all He was as well as all He said, the whole idea of justice which conceived God as a Potentate who governs the world on strict commercial principles of obedience and reward. Still more it was left to Jesus to manifest the rule of God as the direction of a Father whose loving care no ingratitude, disobedience or impiety could ever alienate. Above all it was left to Him to require of us the practical working out of this view by the kindness to the unthankful and evil which is nothing less than the reflection of the Father's perfection.

This principle regulated His whole ministry from the Jordan to Calvary, determining both His thoughts of God and His relations to men. It is the essence of what He means by the Rule or Kingdom of God, and of the meaning of the Cross as the last and highest task in manifesting the good news of this Kingdom.

As the Cross has often been presented, it is not light but gloom, which justifies the passionate hatred of the dark shadow it has cast on life. If it preaches hope at all, it is for another world than this, and that for quite arbitrary reasons. Ruskin speaks in *Modern Painters* of a morbid tendency in Romanism towards the contemplation of bodily pain 'owing to the attribution of saving power to it,' which, he thinks, has left its stain even on the highest Roman painters, so that even Fra Angelico 'always insists weakly on bodily torture, and is unsparing of blood.' But, though it may not have the same visible embodiment, this same insistence, and for the same reason, is by no means confined to the Roman painters. Whensoever the Cross ceases to be light on this world and becomes a device for securing an entrance into another, stress must be laid on the weakness and not the strength, on the agony and not the victory. It ceases to be what it was for Jesus, a surrender to the will of the Father which fulfils all righteousness by manifesting, with unquenchable joy, the eternal and invincible ways of His pardon and love, and becomes mere abjectness of submission amid defeat and agony and death. But how is that a light by which anyone can ever steer, with courage undismayed and hope undimmed, his sure course amid life's rocks and tides?

The true meaning of the Cross is, in the first place, a great denial. It denies emphatically that the end of God's rule in the world is the punishing of the wicked and the rewarding of the righteous. It denies that any illuminating thought of life's meaning, any clear guidance on our own way through life can ever come to us on that principle, for it is not God's way.

The Cross also is a great affirmation that God's purpose is the salvation of His children into His Kingdom, the peace and glory and possessions of which only love can win, and for which only by love can anyone be won.

Let us, whatsoever we do, not accept this merely piously. Was a life in which this view of God's rule shone without ever flickering or showing dim really a light come into the world? Is that truly how God has made the world and how we may possess it? Nothing less is at stake. Do not delude yourselves about the issue. Rather deny it point blank and affirm vehemently that it is an illusion, and that the only reason for doing right is to be well paid for it, and that the way of success for men or nations is to fight well for their own hand. That is far better than to reverence Jesus with our lips and then go and live on the principle of hating those who hate us, and doing to them as we think they would have done to us, and measuring our security by power and our worth by position and human approbation.

If Christ is come a light into the world, it can only be because He manifests the eternal principles of God's rule in it. Seeing they are eternal principles, they cannot be adequately wrought out in time; and if they are such that, in defeat and agony and death, they can still make us more than conquerors, quite obviously defeat and death cannot be the end. Yet eternal principles are not merely for eternity, but there can be no time or place in which they are not valid. If we think there is any time or place in which we may not safely stake our souls on them and entrust to their working all our interests private or public, the idea that we believe in Christ is mere illusion, and, if He is light, we are in darkness.

Let us take a practical illustration. When Jesus tells us that, if we forgive not men their trespasses, neither will our Heavenly Father forgive us, He is not setting a limit to God's mercy. He is merely pointing out a necessity which belongs to the nature of light, the necessity of walking in it if we would not stumble and would catch the promise of its far horizons. He is pointing out that pardoning love, with the esteem of God for His children which gives it meaning, is not merely edifying to contemplate, but is God's actual method of rule outside of which it cannot be well with us. If forgiveness is God's way, we cannot be stronger or better or more secure or have better success by refusing to forgive others.

Let us come back to this, that Jesus is either a light in the world to show us God's mind respecting it, or He is the most mistaken person who ever lived. If He does not reveal God's real way of ruling the world and our own real way of ruling our lives so as to possess the world, the sooner we seek some other guide the better. He is light only if, under the eyelids of its dawn, God's unchanging purpose is beginning at least to appear above the distorting mists and shadows of man's hatreds and violence and selfishness. That is the question; and we answer it, not as we cherish the hope of bliss in another world, but as we find it now the power of an endless life, applicable to all tasks and problems and to all human relations, private and public, national and international, because it displays the certain and undeniable and irresistible principles of God's rule in earth and heaven. If it is light, it must, as light does, lighten all. It can be no light of God unless it show us the right measure of good and the right temper and motive of duty, the right valuation of our fellow-men, the right way of solving our social problems, the right governance of our states, the right and secure relations between peoples. In short, it must illumine for us everything that concerns right thinking and right acting. Its proof is the unveiling of reality, and not merely edifying, comforting and pious feeling: and if it display the way in which God manages His world, it must be the only way in which you, or any other mortal, can ever walk in the world except in darkness.

'If ye know these things, happy are ye if ye do them'; for it is vain to talk of belief in Christ, if worldly cares still devastate your peace, if you think crookedness may be wrong but is the way to success,

if material guarantees for your lives seem a better
security than the witness of a good conscience, if
the service of personal ambition draws you more
than the service even of the unthankful and evil,
if the putting of your enemies into strait-waistcoats
seems a better way of securing the peace of the
world than bringing them to sanity and friendship.

We cannot look at the Master's life and assume
that our path will be smooth and our journey easy.
But, if He often walked in distress, He never walked
in darkness. All righteousness He fulfilled with
perfect discernment and absolute loyalty, using
every opportunity to the full and meeting everyone
with perfect sympathy, understanding and pardon
of all offences. And, if we have anything of His
spirit, what greater blessing could we desire than
thus to abide in the light as He is in the light? What
road should we fear to tread, if we knew it certainly
to be the right way, the way of God's mind in our
troubled time and of God's victory when time's
purposes shall have been fulfilled?

Most of us perhaps, like the prophets, feel that
we live in a time that is darkness and not light.
Confusion and distress fall upon our spirits as we
realise that we do not know even how to begin to
cast out the devils of hatred and suspicion, to feed
the hungry and minister to the desolate, to introduce
a new reign of brotherhood and peace. But is it
because light has not come into the world or because
evil passions and worldly ambitions blind our eyes

to it, and unworthy fears hinder us from trusting its guidance? Might we not soon see our way, were our one fixed purpose to walk in the light, to see in Jesus God's absolute mind about life and our duty in it? Light makes just one demand—faith to walk in it. That means ruthless sincerity and, above all, sincerity with our own empty, gushing, unreal words and forms. Nor can aught else be the supreme demand, if Jesus has really come a light into our world and if we are so to believe in Him that we shall no longer abide in darkness.

VII

A PANACEA

JOHN xiv. 8. 'Lord, shew us the Father, and it sufficeth us.'

PHILIP's question is usually esteemed a mere crude misunderstanding. Into the midst of his Master's discourse on the deepest things of faith he strikes in with a gross demand for the help of sight. With his natural eyes in some way he would see God. Then he would be satisfied, but not till then.

Yet there are reasons for pausing before accepting this estimate. Philip was a Jew who had been taught from childhood that no man had seen God at any time; he had been chosen one of the twelve, surely for something more than common spiritual insight; and, in Peter's words, he had companied with them all the time the Lord Jesus went in and out among them, surely to some profit.

Nor is there any suggestion of pain, not to speak of rebuke, in the Master's reply, as there must have been had the meaning of His own words been grossly perverted from seeing the Father with the eye of faith into seeing Him with the eye of flesh. Nor would the misunderstanding have been only of this teaching, but would have marked the Master's overwhelming failure to impress aright in any way even His own most intimate followers.

Yet Jesus merely appeals to their fellowship together, which, on this supposition, had been so utterly fruitless; and the substance of what He says is to assure Philip that he already possesses what he thinks he needs. 'He that hath seen me hath seen the Father, and how sayest thou then, Shew us the Father?'

The key to Philip's meaning is the words, 'it sufficeth us,' because the measure of his behest is the terrible experience for which it was to suffice. The shepherd was to be smitten and the sheep scattered abroad. The presence of the Master, which had been hitherto all their strength, was to be withdrawn. Like lone children they were to be pushed out into the night where faces scowled in the dim light and dangers lurked in every shadow, and the storm gathered, and where, they had just been told, the bravest of them would quail and utterly come short in loyalty and truth.

Jesus had gone on to say, 'Let not your heart be troubled'; but, after what He had told them, it must have seemed like asking the impossible. If they were thus to be tried and to fail in the trial, how could their hearts be other than overwhelmed by trouble? Could they have been assured of playing a worthy part, they might have steeled their hearts to bear, but, with even that hope denied them, was it not mockery to say, 'Let not your heart be troubled'? If, nevertheless, Philip could say, 'It sufficeth us,' surely he had found a solid ground of faith and seen a great vision of hope in what Jesus had gone on to say.

'Ye believe in God.' Yes, they could all reply, they always had believed in God. The future, they knew, could not be wholly dark, if the last word was with God and not with man.

Yet for their own private lives God seemed too remote to be a present succour and too much the embodiment of mere righteousness to be a consolation in their sin and failure. Moreover, belief depended too much on abstractions and probabilities to sustain them in face of evils so real, so visible. Thus for what actually lay before them, no one could say belief in God would suffice.

But Jesus continued, I have meant for you another knowledge of God and another way of knowing. He that hath seen me, hath seen the Father—a Father in a home with many mansions, one of them reserved for Peter with his triple denial.

Then, like a flash, it came home to Philip that here was a security which would suffice even for the day when the Master should be gone from their midst, their company be broken up, their cause discredited and each of them left standing alone against a hostile world, bearing heavy responsibilities and with grave failures to be made good. Could he, like Jesus, see the Father in all this world of time and chance, tracing His love in every adversity, hearing His word of forgiveness in every passion of hatred, and looking, as he had looked in the

Master's face, for recovery even in remorse and the shipwreck of human confidence, it would suffice for all that might befall.

Philip's prayer is then no cry of a darkened and material mind, a mind determined to walk by sight and not by faith, a mind belonging to the adulterous generation that sought after a sign, but is the deep and spiritual utterance of a heart knowing its own weakness and discerning its true succour. And our Lord's answer, though in the form of a question, is a tender and gracious assurance that, in their fellowship together, Philip's prayer had been already answered, and that he need no more ask for what he already possessed.

Philip, like so many of the rest of us, was in trouble only because he had failed to discover and use the privileges he already enjoyed. As argument could at best have confirmed the belief in God, Jesus simply led him back to their experience together. Then Philip knew that he had already seen a vision which had transformed for him the world. Cloud and lake and tillage field and wayside flower became eloquent of the Father's care; the equal rain told of the Father's love and pardon to His erring sons; the play of children and the daily tasks of men and life's joys and sorrows mirrored the Father's Kingdom; even the faces of the sinful and lost were in the Father's image. What was yet lacking in the revelation a day or two would complete, when he would see the will of the Father done in agony of body and soul, but in a spirit which transformed every evil which life could pour upon the head of the righteous into the patient, pardoning love of the Father.

Even to believe in God seemed to many in days of desolation and slaughter an impossible achievement. Yet only by belief in God is it possible for any one to burn through an evil time for his brethren, as was said of Cromwell, 'like a fiery pillar of hope.'

In the might of armies and the policies of statesmen our confidence never can be more than straw which blazes up in the dry and favouring breeze and dies down in the lashing storm. If there is no God, we are, in face of unjust might and blind accident, without hope in the world. This we have learned as we never knew in a pleasant, easy, prosperous time when things went so well with us that a world without God seemed as secure as a world with God, and belief in a benevolent Being behind it was as easy as it was unimportant. When a world without God is not benevolent at all; when it is a ghastly slaughter-house caused by insane ambitions, and brutal violences, and base lust of gain; when it may be subjected to the triumph of cunning and strength, with destruction of all that is tender and beautiful and human and free and just; when the issue may be a cowering, servile, withered race to people a graveyard of a world, the value of a world with God begins to appear. In face of such possibilities we would rejoice to believe in a

God even of the sternest righteousness. 'To Him,' says the Psalmist, 'belongeth mercy, for He rendereth to every man according to his works.' As we look out upon the works of iniquity, we can understand how judgment may be mercy, not only to the sufferer, but even to the sinner.

But also, when we really face such issues of possible human evil, we know that, in spite of everything, we believe in God. We do not believe that policies and armies finally determine the destiny of humanity, and that the true and gracious and holy things have no might, and that the last word of wisdom can be statecraft and the last weight in the scales of the future iron shards. We know that, however long our patience may still be tried, the end is not yet, and that it will not be according to the violence of man, but according to the purpose of God. In spite of all, nay, because of all, we believe in God, and it means the difference between a world with our souls hardly bested and hungry and a world in which hope maketh not ashamed.

But who in such days could say, Let us believe in God and it sufficeth us? Who, indeed, can say it in any day? The might of evil is too visible and near for mere belief; we share in it too deeply to trust only the final triumph of righteousness; our conflict is too immediate and personal to allow us to wait patiently the working of God: the urgency of the present task does not allow us to judge it only by God's final end. But in face of the true reality of war, our need, if not greater, is more insistent.

As of all events in time, war concerns the hopes and fears, the joys and sorrows, the sublime thoughts and the mean, the fellowships and the desolations of human hearts. We learned to think in millions of what was lived through by individuals, and even of the millions we lost count. Yet each soldier on either side left a useful, peaceful avocation and a cheerful fireside, and his mother or his wife, his sisters or his children hung about his neck as he departed; and now he moulders in the chalk of Flanders, where no man knows, and his chair he will never fill again, and there will be a void in the hearts that loved him to the end of time. And how shall we measure the sacred associations of homes going up in flames, and women and children fleeing wildly amid shell and bullet that pursue retreating armies, or mothers watching their children dying while hunger gnaws at their own vitals. Nor may we forget the dreary days of captivity, the terrible pressure which drives reason from her throne, or the men who must face life again, maimed and broken.

For all that agony of body and spirit what would suffice? Have we any answer except Philip's? Lord, show us the Father, without whom none of these many dead have fallen, none of these many homes been made desolate, none of these frames quivered in pain, none of these bitter tears been shed. Show us

that the sighing of the prisoner has come up into His
ear, that He has put the tears of the widow and the
orphan into His bottle, that He has led the blind by
a way that they knew not, that He has truly borne
our griefs and carried our sorrows.

The wages of sin must be death; evil must work
out its own disaster. God's gifts for life, being
misused, become messengers of death; the society
He meant for His Kingdom can be turned into the
tyranny of darkness. Human responsibility can
prove its appalling significance by working evil;
the brotherhood of man can be turned into organised
destruction. Yet if we could see that it is the very
reverence of the Father for His own image in His
children which suffers them, in the exercise of the
responsibility He has given them, to work these
calamities, but that, in their evil-doing, He continues
kind, even to the unthankful and evil, and that there
is no soul of man He does not pity and love, and
for which He has not an eternal purpose worthy of
all the discipline of life's agony and death's despair,
would it not suffice us?

Argument at best would help us to believe in
God, and even then only with the fainting cry,
'Lord, I believe, help thou my unbelief.' Would
we see the Father, is there any way except to follow
Him who set His face steadfastly to go up to
Jerusalem, there to tread the winepress alone in
agony and bloody sweat, and be despised and
rejected of men, and robed with purple in mockery

and crowned with thorns, and be nailed to the Cross
of shame, and suffer all the pangs mortal frame can
undergo, and all the darkness that can fall upon
the fainting spirit, to reveal the Father in every
horror of body and soul that man can undergo, in
doing His will, obedient unto death?

In these days still He too may be going before in
solemn silence, with the shadow of events darkening
His brow, and we may be amazed and as we follow
be afraid; and a heavy fear may be upon us that we
too may fail Him in the great day of decision. But
even so we may be seeing the Father and learning
that neither life nor death nor any created thing shall
separate us from His love, and that in the end we shall
be more than conquerors through Him who loved us,
and that our Father's house has still many mansions
into which shall be garnered all we have sown in
tears, whither we shall come bringing our sheaves
with us, ay, even if they have in them the tares and
thistles of our doubts and our denials.

VIII

A DISTRESSED MIND AND UNTROUBLED HEART

JOHN xiv. 1. 'Let not your heart be troubled: ye believe in God, believe also in me.'

MARK xiv. 33. 'And he taketh with him Peter and James and John, and began to be greatly amazed, and sore troubled.'

THESE incidents both belong to the few hours between the defection of Judas and the actual betrayal. In both Jesus is alone with His disciples, facing the same terrible prospect of His own agony and their desertion. But this nearness in time and similarity in outward situation only render more amazing the contrast in inward mood. In one, the disciples are filled with dismay, while Jesus is calm and assured, with abundant peace, not alone for His own need, but also for all who trust Him: in the other, His dearest companions are dull of apprehension and heavy with sleep, while Jesus, in His dismay, vainly casts Himself upon their sympathy, confessing that His soul is exceeding sorrowful, even unto death.

The whole difference has been ascribed to John's peculiar view of Jesus. But he also admits that Jesus was troubled in spirit, or, as we should say, in mind; and he is not alone in thinking that Jesus came to give peace. Mark, no more than John, doubted that Jesus gave victory over fear as well as over sin. And, apart from either, faith in Jesus as a refuge in distress has never been separated from the knowledge that He himself passed through the depths of dismay. He was acquainted with grief in His soul as well as in His life, being no more shielded from its distress in mind than in body. Nor would He avail for our need, had He not, in every sense, undergone our experience.

Suffering, nevertheless, is not victory. That depends wholly on how it is endured. Had Jesus faced His trials, as many descriptions of Him might lead us to suppose, as a soft, sensitive person, shrinking from life's rough experiences, forgetful of its joys and brooding much on its miseries, keenly but passively enduring its cruelties and its wrongs, He could have been no Captain in any warfare. Nor is He so represented in the Gospels.

Even the Crucifixion must be wrongly conceived when the dying Christ is pictured with nothing in His face except abject, awful, unresisting anguish. He must have died as He had lived, as the greatest of all fighters in the battle between light and darkness, life and death, heaven and hell. However His mortal flesh and human spirit were broken by agony, as His heart did not turn back, there must have shone on His dying face the glory and peace of victory. Paul, at least, could speak of it as a conflict triumphantly maintained to the end, the pain endured, consciously and willingly, and the shame despised, actively and forcefully, not in passive misery, but for the joy set before Him.

If, throughout His life, Jesus was a man of sorrows of a depth we may never fathom, His pure spirit must also have had joys to which we cannot soar. We catch glimpses of it in His delight in nature and children and the ways of man, in His supreme insight into the only book He perhaps had much opportunity of reading, in the quietness and absence of hurry amid the tumult of His days, and above all in the serenity and security of His fellowship with the Father. He nursed no trouble and cherished no grief. He knew no ills which are only evil because we think them so. He brooded on no fears and anticipated no troubles. His days were not darkened even by the Cross, till He stood in its shadow. Life He met with a hardened body and disciplined mind, which enabled Him to take privations, dangers, oppositions, misrepresentations, as what Chalmers the missionary used to call, 'the pepper and salt of life.' Having the joy of a great cause and the concentration of a great purpose, He was never the victim of trivial anxieties or mean worries or small annoyances, to which men are exposed by unworthy aims and ungirt loins.

In reaction from the mistaken gloom of former views, Jesus has more recently been pictured as a cheerful, delightful person, the incarnation of geniality, with an easy, humorous way of disposing of difficulties, and with charming grace of manner and superiority to all austerity. Being a very human picture, there is no temptation to make Jesus mentally any more than physically superior to sufferings, either by impassiveness, as Christian Science, or by omnipotence, as some theologies. If physical evil has no reality, neither has moral; and this view makes plain that our Lord's solution, whatever it may have been, had nothing to do with denying the appalling reality of either. Yet, even with this recognition of graver issues, while it is of value for reminding us of important elements in the life of Jesus which have too often been overlooked, does this presentation altogether do justice to the intensity of His conflict and the absoluteness of His demands? Above all is it adequate to the dark, tremendous judgment of men and things, through which He travels to victory? After no manner, not even the manner of geniality, does He hold out any hope of peace with life as good in itself and by itself.

On this immediate judgment of life Buddha's view of it as misery is true; and Jesus knew this better than Buddha. The higher the life, the more responsive the feeling and the intenser the sympathies; and, therefore, the more it is exposed to pain.

Even of bodily suffering this is true. A higher mind creates for itself a finer organisation with keener sensibilities, while a coarser mind has duller sensations. As Carlyle puts it, 'Stupidity and a good digestion can face much.' Even an excitable mind in a high-strung body has ways of escaping anguish not open to a mind of perfect balance and sanity in a body under perfect discipline and healthy control. We read of martyrs with feelings so exalted as to make them unconscious even of the flames; and some have argued that Jesus was less heroic than they because nothing of the kind shielded Him from agony.

But it is neither the bravest nor the most experienced soldier whom excitement renders impervious to danger. For this way of escape Jesus was too strong and self-possessed, too inflexibly resolute in facing reality, and, above all, too familiar with conflict. Thus, neither by hardness nor by exaltation, was anything human flesh or spirit could endure ever softened for Him. Nor can we realise what it meant for Him to endure to the end in fulfilling all righteousness, unless we perceive with what clear consciousness and with what revolt of His healthy, sane, sensitive nature, He faced it.

And to this agony of body consider what was added of anguish of mind. Though it could not silence His prayer that they might be forgiven, the hatred of those He would have saved wrapped Him like a flame. Though their iniquity was directed against Himself, the disasters His persecutors were preparing for themselves and their children wrung His soul with grief. Though it could not make Him fail to pity their distress and weakness, the desertion of his disciples left Him a lonely object of universal scorn. Finally, though it could not sap His confidence in commending His spirit into the hands of His Father, as body and mind were broken in agony, He felt forsaken of God.

In those hours miseries were heaped upon Him such as neither Buddha, nor any other mortal, ever experienced, or perhaps had the strength of mind consciously to endure. Yet He drank this bitter cup to the dregs as appointed by the love of the Father who is altogether good, and as, therefore, in the deepest sense also good. Through the most utter outward defeat, the most cruel and shameful execution devised for the basest criminals, with agony in every nerve and black darkness upon His mind, He yet dreamt of no Nirvana, no cessation of being and pain. He did not even dwell on Heaven as bliss after this warfare should have been accomplished, but the joy set before Him was a present as well as an invincible good, for which He was glad to live and ready to die. From the work given Him to do He never turned His eyes, and nothing necessary for accomplishing it ever ceased to be a joy.

But, you may ask, was not every element of joy, whether of duty done or of serving His brethren or of manifesting His Father, blotted out when He uttered the despairing cry, 'My God, my God, why hast Thou forsaken me'?

To many it has appeared that this shadowing of the face of the Father may not be ascribed merely to the agony of the Crucifixion, without regarding the faith of Jesus as weaker than that of such human martyrs as Stephen whose last hours were illumined by more than mortal vision of heavenly succour. They, therefore, think it necessary to find some other explanation: and two explanations have specially found favour.

The first ascribes it to a supernatural, collective, representative heaping of the world's sin upon His head, under which, as our substitute, He endured such a shadow of the wrath of God as hid from Him the Father's face.

But the world's sin is a moral and personal responsibility, and not a massed collective shadow. Nor has such a way of solving a moral problem any agreement with the mind of the Father as Jesus revealed it. Above all, this view has not a vestige of support from anything in the narrative, though, if it had been a reality, it ought to have been the dominant feature.

The other explains the words as an unfinished quotation from the Twenty-second Psalm. Though His dying lips could fashion no more words, they show that His heart was dwelling on such assurances as, 'They trusted in Thee and were not ashamed,' on such prayers as, 'Be not far off, O Lord: O Thou, my succour, haste Thee to my help,' and on such promises as, 'Let your heart live forever. All the

ends of the earth shall remember and turn unto
the Lord.' Yet the words are there by themselves,
and it is difficult to suppose that those who reported
them thought them other than a cry from the
depths; and when we recall how, even as He
entered the shadow, He had acknowledged His
soul sore troubled even unto death, we cannot be
sure that they were not, just by themselves, the dark
centre of His conscious thought. It is the only saying on the Cross the Evangelists thought necessary
to hand down in the original Aramaic tongue. They
added neither expansion nor explanation, thinking
either that it needed none or was beyond it. And, if
we take it as they did, must it not be as a cry
from the great darkness which had wrapped for the
moment His anguished mind, to which we must add
nothing and in which we must explain nothing, but
accept them simply as expressing the most terrible
experience of His awful ordeal. And had He escaped
that moment of desolation, would He have truly
sounded all the depths of man's darkness and loneliness and desolation?

And, yet, when all this has been said, we have
not wholly done away with the significance of the
fact that this cry of dismay is a quotation from a
Psalm of assurance and hope, for there is nothing
more marvellous in the mind than the penumbra
of light which may surround the blackest centre of
eclipse. Does it not show that the sun of His faith still
shone behind, His heart still at peace though His

mind was overshadowed? God was still the great reality and was still His God, and though like a child in the night He had lost His hand, like a child also He stretched forth His arm, to find again its strengthening hold.

In what is merely the human spirit there is a breaking point of endurance, as well as in what is merely the mortal body. To ascribe to John a definite and absolute distinction between the heart which the faith of Christ can guard from trouble, and the mind from which it could not be excluded even by Jesus Himself, may be too much of a refinement. Definite and absolute walls of separation in our nature, we, at least, cannot discover. Yet, in our strange, complex, closely inter-related being, there must be some sharp dividing line between our mortal and our immortal part. This latter is what the New Testament calls the heart; and its chrysalis, both of body and of mind, may include more of our nature than we realise. Yet we are not wholly without experience of an utter breaking of our powers which are revealing moments of something in us neither to be broken nor dismayed.

A soldier after years spent in the hottest parts of India went in winter straight to France. There he spent fifty-two hours in a trench filled with freezing water, and under a fire which scarce permitted of any movement. He was in the hospital suffering, from the effect of it, days shot through with intense pain and nights of fitful snatches of sleep broken by almost unendurable pangs. After he had told of the horrible long nightmare of it, he added: "But I am glad to have gone through it; I am glad to have lived to have this experience; I am glad to know what man can endure." He did not mean that he was proud to have borne so much now that it was over. It was still very far from being over. Nor was there in his mind the dimmest thought of boasting. What he did mean was that he had passed through one of life's great unveiling experiences which had revealed to him, away down in his soul, deeper than his heavily distressed conscious mind, something which had not been troubled. This it is which may rest unshaken on the Eternal, even while all conscious thought is blackness of desolation.

All else in our nature can be broken, and the breaking of it with few—and these not the strongest —is with ecstasy. The common experience is like the Master's own, of falling backwards into the abyss, with all supports of God and man removed from under us. Yet this is a thing wholly of nature, as much as the empty rent shell from which the butterfly has escaped; and that our Lord shared it with us is the final proof that He fully partook of our humanity.

But, while He suffered without and within all we can endure, and that with a specially poignant distress, He never turned His face from life, or resented God's appointment for Him in it, or thought it aimless or senseless misery, or desired to escape from it into a passionless existence. Though for the moment His conscious thought was a black desolation, deep in His heart was the shining light of a psalm of hope and assurance and the turning of man to God, the joy of it immediately blazing up into confident surrender of His spirit into the Father's hands. And where else may our faith plant its last tottering footstep as we ascend through the storm and darkness of time to the light and peace of the life eternal; where else can we rest assured that there is no ill over which the Cross is not God's victory, and no way so dark as to be deprived of His peace, except in that dismayed but finally triumphant question?

In the prosperous days when even Christian people could think of God's peace as something akin to worldly ease, we used to be told of a higher faith which would save us from all distress, at least of spirit. But where do we read of it in the life of any prophet or saint or hero of faith? In the life of the Master Himself was He made immune by faith any more than by hardness or by omnipotence? In the intensity of their conflict the greatest of His followers spoke of the righteous scarcely being saved, of being saved yet so as by fire, of coming through only after succumbing in battles both of the flesh and the spirit; and the Master Himself did not escape dismay and the shadow of a great darkness.

When we begin to define and explain, we too

easily descend to the things merely of the mind and
fail to rise to the issues of the heart. Then what
we say of Christ as power to make us, in face even
of suffering and weakness and darkness, glad to live
and ready to die, is often crude and always inadequate, giving a wrong and superficial and immediate and even material impression of what we take
life's real good, as well as death's real hope, to be.
But the heart can know what the mind cannot explain,
and it knows that, even if the flesh be crushed and
the spirit broken, it itself may not be troubled, but
can rejoice unwaveringly still to live, and, as part of
life, to die, confidently commending itself, even in its
rebellion and weakness and darkness, into God's
hands, knowing that no evil, no defeat, no despair
can hinder life from being the joyful gift of the Most
High to the children He has made in His own
image, and that, through it, they may realise His
blessed will in victory and peace, and find death the
last and highest triumph of life.

IX

THE PARADOX OF THE WORLD

Romans viii. 28. 'And we know that all things work together for good to them that love God, to them who are the called according to his purpose.'

There is a method in literature by which thoughts which are dominant in a writer's mind are made apparent, which is known as "the method of recurrences and fervours." That is to say, we judge by the frequency and intensity with which the idea is repeated in various forms. On this test the thought in our text must have been, in a high degree, both central and continuous in the mind of the Apostle. Here it is obviously the intensest expression of a very intense mood. And, when he expresses the same thought in other ways, it is always the same. 'With Christ God freely gives us all things.' 'All things are yours, for ye are Christ's and Christ is God's.' 'All things are of God who reconciled us to Himself through Jesus Christ.' Nor could an experience of Christ which thus gave meaning and value to all experience do other than rule his thoughts and colour all his emotions.

Yet the world in itself was to him still an evil dominion, and life in it was not less than before a burden and a sorrow; and he is well aware that, on the ordinary estimate, what he says is nothing more than sheer paradox. Unless it is seen as an illumination, it must seem an absurdity. He knows that he is making the most unlikely affirmation, about the most unlikely people, and for the most unlikely reason. But he also knows that what he calls reconciliation turns it from an incredible paradox into the most triumphant certainty. At enmity with God, all the world is against us; at peace with Him, all of it is on our side.

1. IT IS THE MOST UNLIKELY AFFIRMATION
'We know that all things work together for good.'

The utmost that the most cheerful, hopeful, optimistic human opinion has ventured to maintain about the world is that it is, for those who know how to make the best of it, pretty good upon the whole. Even when it has been called the best of all possible worlds, a large, uncomfortable margin has to be allowed for as inexplicable.

But the world, in this sense, is not, for the Apostle, good even in a moderate degree. It is the place into which we come naked and alone, and out of which again we go naked and alone. All our journey through it, defend ourselves as we may, we remain open to assault; and, surround ourselves with friends as we may, we are alone in the depths of our hearts. To trust in anything working for our good in the way of mere possession and material security is to make a god of this world: and no other delusion so shuts us off from real trust in God or from any need of learning His mind. Paul even affirms that his gospel never is hid except as this kind of trust, which he calls the god of this world, has blinded men's eyes. To him, as to his Lord, the ruler of this world—the world so conceived—is the Father of Lies, the supreme source of all self-delusion. To build our hopes on the promise of it is to prove ourselves fools, because it does not work even imperfectly, and much less all of it together, for good.

Faith is not blindness to life's uncertainties and miseries. Until faith in providence as mere beneficence breaks down, the faith which reconciles us to God in face of every conceivable evil cannot arise. But, then, nothing whatsoever in the world is omitted from what works together for good.

This does not, however, mean that all life is forthwith made happy or in any way good in itself. Creation still groans and travails, and those who have God's peace in their souls do not least share in its pain. The good for which the world works is not the world itself. It no more makes the world good by itself than ploughing, as mere tearing up the soil, would be good without the harvest, or quarrying, as mere breaking up stones, would be good without building them into houses. So with experience. Only in view of its final purpose is it good at all, but, directed to that end, none of it can finally be hurtful. For this higher good it all works together, so that, however calamitous in itself, it is blessed in its effect. Nor is it good merely by the preponderance of the pleasant things we cherish, but the unpleasant things we shun have equally their place.

Health and prosperity and youth and repute and friendship and good success we are all ready to admit as on our side. But now the claim is that they are not a whit more friendly to our lasting and supremely worthy good than the most painful, most uncertain, most calamitous events. This was the victory which overcame the world, and, as it left nothing that could be against us, it manifestly was a crowning triumph.

The change is so great that all things become new. The world is a new creation. Yet the only really new element is the discovery of God's unchanging meaning in it and purpose with it. It is new only as a lesson is new when it ceases to burden us as a task and begins to stir our imagination as poetry, or as a message is new when, read by the right code, it changes from chaotic words to rational meaning.

The worldly view is one code, and the Christian view is another. The former works with pleasures and possessions and what is usually regarded as the good things of life. With the best effort, the result is mixed and contradictory, yet, so long as people have health and ease and fair prosperity, and life's drift seems to be according to the meanings they desire, they persist with great confidence. But there come times when life on such terms cannot be made to signify anything; and if our code is wrong, that is a gain. To be forced to admit that our interpretation is utter confusion is the first necessity. Wherefore, a mood of dark distress may be far nearer a Christian hope than cheerful, well-fed, unthinking satisfaction with our lot. Hence the gain of days like our own when every doctrine of Providence which is based on ideas of ease and happiness or any kind of beneficence has come to grief amid a horror of thick darkness.

Nevertheless many persist with the old code, little modified; and our worst danger is that we should start afresh with merely a slight revision. Such for example is the idea of a finite God doing His best to interline with good this general devil's manuscript of blind mechanical indifference, for it still works with our ordinary notion of good, and does not go on to ask the vital question which concerns the good God purposes to achieve.

Reconciliation to God is just agreement with His mind about this good. What it is appears in Jesus Christ. He is the Second Adam—all God intends man to be. So supremely is this God's mind that He is the fullness of God: and so completely does it sum up the purpose of all God's doings that in Him are hid all the treasures of wisdom and knowledge. This amazingly exalted language rests on the experience of finding in Christ a consistent, certain, complete and blessed meaning for all experience, through the kind of good God intends it all to serve, and in view of which none of it is imperfect or superfluous.

This power to reconcile us to God in all His way with us is summed up in the Cross, wherein every form of evil is made to work for good. Even death, with every conceivable accompaniment of shame and agony and visible defeat, is turned into the doing of God's will and the revelation of His pardoning love and the manifestation and victory of His righteousness and peace. Having found there the good which alone is of incomparable value, we learn also that the worst as well as the best must serve it.

This does not mean that there are no evils to be shunned. What we may shun is not appointed. Still less does it mean that there is nothing to be altered and nothing to be opposed. What in that case is appointed is the duty of altering or opposing. Nor does it deny that we live under a system which works out general consequences affecting equally saint and sinner. But it affirms that, behind the inevitable and the natural, there is a power wholly different from brute force and relentless law and blind working. The world is still an order, but it is the order of God's household. Its very quality is that it is determined by the needs of His children. Yet it is no less an order, because their first need is to find their profit in the general good and not to wish to be distinguished in outward favours from their brethren. The very heart of the discovery is the spirit which forgives and bears and forbears, and which no longer judges life by the narrow mind which would apportion rewards by our measure of merit. Its good is not of that material kind, nor is it apportioned in that hard legal way, but is, through Christ, a total change of all our views of good and of all our ways of seeking it and of all our relations to one another in the enjoyment of it. In one sense it is altogether above and beyond the world and all its glory, being a glory of God, not only for our own souls, but for the perfect household of God wherein they are blessed. Yet it is in no sense apart from the world and its right uses, just as the harvest is above and beyond the seed-time, yet is in no sense separate or apart, but is the sole meaning and value of all its labours.

2. It is the most unlikely affirmation, about the most unlikely persons

'To them who are the called according to his purpose.'

If it takes a heroic effort of faith to believe that all things work together for any one, how much more difficult is it to believe that they so work for those who are devoted to the highest. Surely the nobler and greater and more spiritual the purpose, the worse do things serve those who pursue it. Socrates was rewarded with a cup of poison, Dante with exile, the inventor of printing with being thought in

league with the devil, the founder of modern
science with imprisonment as a heretic, and many
pioneers of freedom with the scaffold or the stake.
Many have had the same experience as Paul himself. For what he wrought with his hands some kind
of meagre living-wage was accorded him, but for
what he wrought with his mind and heart he had
only vituperation and stoning and imprisonment
and finally martyrdom. Above all, how did things
work for Him whom, on Paul's view, it ought to
have served best of all? He had nowhere to lay His
head and was despised and rejected. His final
payment was the Cross—a shameful, agonising,
appalling execution as a criminal. Yet, in face of
all this obvious loss of worldly advantage, the
Apostle maintains that the world belongs to those
who have a definite sense of a call to a divinely
appointed task, that all of it works for them, and
none of it belongs to any one else or works to any
one else's profit, and that, finally, it never served
any one absolutely except Him in whom God's
purpose was perfectly realised, the person whom
of all men it seemed to serve worst.

A call according to God's purpose is not an exclusively Christian experience. Every prophet had
it, and no greater accounts of it exist than those
given by Isaiah and Jeremiah. It is not even limited
to the Bible. Where any one is brought to realise
that his own purpose in life is nothing, and is led,
regardless of loss or trouble or human disapproval,

to follow a higher, we may not deny that there is a call of God.

But the Apostle's call was through Jesus Christ: and it was the same with those to whom he spoke. As an experience, it was not different from a prophetic call, or any summons which made one's own purposes subordinate to God's. But Jesus meant both a new sense of God's purpose for all and a new relation to it of all our ordinary human ways. Before Him, God's call had been limited to a few great and specially endowed souls, and only for unusual and conspicuous tasks, mostly at some great crisis in human affairs. But in Christ the call came to all kinds of humble Christian folk to serve God's high purpose in all kinds of common ways.

Yet Christ's call is thus for all and embraces all things, not because it is lower, but because it is higher than any other. No purpose could be higher than to be God's son in whom He is well pleased, nor any life greater than that which manifests the Father. But a light set in the heavens is not thereby set apart from us. On the contrary it is thereby made available for all. It is not like a lighthouse by which you can only steer great ships, but like the pole-star by which the wayfarer in the valley and the shepherd on the hill can guide their steps. Select souls for special achievement we may not be able to be, but the higher purpose of being sons of God we all can have. Then every experience which concerns this high relationship is forthwith

exalted. Where in these common tasks we forget ourselves to seek first God's Kingdom and His righteousness, there is supremely the Divine service.

What the Apostle says he knows is that those who
are thus called are the people, the only people, who
possess the world, and find all things in it work
for good. The very secret of all profitable use of
life is just to abandon the expectation that it ever
was designed to forward persons devoted to material
and merely worldly purposes, with no higher ends
than gain or pleasure or pride of place, and to discern that naturally the only ends it could have been
designed to serve are God's.

On a superficial and immediate judgment this is
obviously quite untrue. The higher your aim, the
more difficult it is to get life to work for it, and
the more all the powers of the world and of society
are massed against it. To be called, with the unwavering devotion which alone is God's call, to serve
truth and beauty and holiness, which alone is God's
purpose, will make you more likely to be poor than
rich, to be hated than approved, to be despised than
praised. The more utterly your call is as your
Master's, the more your destiny is likely to be as His:
nor has He ever asked you to follow Him on other
terms.

But only the very thoughtless can take life at
its face value. Reflection challenges all our hasty
judgments, and more particularly about those who
make the most of life. Are they so certainly those

who are most efficient for their own purposes of winning the world's material rewards? Their ambitions may be tangible, but do they prove satisfying? Do they fill the heart's deepest needs? In the end for what do all things work together except to reduce such achievements and every hope and trust built on them to dust? And, on the contrary, do those who are called according to God's purpose so certainly draw blanks in life's lottery? Is aspiration, or hope, or inward peace, or the sense of God's approval, or any spiritual issue no compensation for loss and pain and long delay? Many people are always confident of being right when they are arguing on mean and material grounds. But are they? Whence comes this universal sense among all prophetic souls that the God, according to whose purpose they are called, possesses the earth and its fullness? What makes them speak in such exalted terms of the ease of His power, as, for example, taking up the isles as a very little thing? Why did the Greatest, whom outwardly life served worst, think that in His hard life and shameful, terrible death, He manifested a Father who numbers our hairs, frees us from care and enables us to set all fears at defiance? How could those who followed Him find that from God are all things and unto Him are all things, that they may be ours, without limit and without exception?

Practical issues are never tested by argument,

and if this is a true experience, must we not revise our notions of those who really possess the world and find all things theirs?

3. IT IS THE MOST UNLIKELY AFFIRMATION ABOUT THE MOST UNLIKELY PERSONS, AND FOR THE MOST UNLIKELY REASON

'To them that love God.'

If we follow our outward and obvious judgment of life, we could hardly conceive anything more incredible, more utterly paradoxical. Is it not certain that the people who win the world's possessions and the world's ease and the world's honours, for whose good all things appear to work, are those who look well after their own interests, and concentrate their powers on getting on, undistracted by a conscience very sensitive towards God or very considerate towards man? Love to God, with its troublesome scrupulousness and absorption in self-forgetting interests, and its distracting sympathy with those who are ridden down in competition, and its calls to linger behind to help those who have fallen by the way, is surely life's heaviest handicap. In our day there are many who openly declare that it is a condition to be observed only at the cost of prompt and utter insolvency.

Yet here is Paul maintaining that to love God is the only condition on which we ever can be solvent on any permanent or essential issue: and he certainly did not seem to come short in realising the extent of the demands it makes, whether of sensitiveness towards God or of considerateness for His children. Moreover, he seems to have staked confidently his own life upon the issue in the most impressive and heroic way, in such a way at least as gives him a right to summon us to reflection.

But the moment you reflect, you must, on the most external judgment, have some doubts of the real value of selfish success. How often is what is selfishly earned hurtfully spent, what is selfishly hoarded a burden of anxiety and an enslaving to greed, what is selfishly enjoyed mere food for ever more insatiate desire! Finally, all gain of this kind may at any time leave its possessor; and it is certain that he must leave it.

But, still further, it does not require very profound reflection to see that no merely external judgment can measure life's most valuable blessings. On no other matter is the danger of indulging in platitude quite so great, yet it is not a platitude that the soul lives by vision of the truth and is enriched by the gentle and gracious and beautiful things of character and has its only true social success in the fellowship of the wise and the good.

At times when you are sensitive and sore, you have no doubt been tempted to think that nothing equips for the battle like hardness of heart. Yet it is not the rigid bough which weathers the storm, nor the granite cliff which encroaches upon the sea, nor the heart hardened to bone which stands the strain of living. On deeper reflection must you not find the mood in which you envy the hard hearted to be hasty and shallow? On the contrary, do not they miss all that is best? Is it not just the love which ever draws the heart upwards and keeps it tender and sensitive and responsive to all around it, the love to God which loves all He seeks and all for whom He seeks it, that is the one supreme condition for getting out of life its highest good and finding the true meaning of all experience? And surely love alone can face all experience, making no selection from it of what is easy and pleasant and profitable, but finding also pain and conflict and opprobrium and death itself turned by its own alchemy to serve its own uses.

This the Apostle says we know. Knowledge seems a strong expression for our faltering, dubious, broken trust that somehow the highest is the surest. But he too admits that it is fragmentary, like a blurred image in a mirror of rusty steel. And he must more frequently speak of it as faith, a mount of vision up which knowledge climbs with trembling steps. Yet, then, he says still more boldly, We see. Faith is never to him a mere exalted state of feeling, a mere emotional persuasion, but is always insight into the world as God has actually made it and the real purpose for which He uses it.

Faith works, Paul says, by love. But this does not mean love as an emotion. It means that love is life's deepest reality. Very imperfectly we may know it, but it wholly knows us and succours us in all our ways. And the simple issue is that, when we know the great purpose love has called us to, and, through Jesus Christ, accept it as our own, and are at one with God in seeking to realise it, we know also that no trial or difficulty or distress or aught the world can bring against us can ever shake our confidence that love directs our whole life toward that high end and can justify all it ever required us either to suffer or to do.

This knowledge concerns, not our emotions, but God's rule. Either God so directs the world that it serves only material ends, and then the way to use it is efficient direction of our energies to self-interest; or He has made it to serve spiritual ends, and then the way to use it is by utter devotion to His purpose, in a love to Him which meets all trials with patience and does all duty with humility, and which issues in reverence and consideration and loyalty for all His children. If one is right, the other is wrong; and there is no middle way.

But remember you must choose by what you know to be true and not merely by what you feel to be edifying. It concerns the real nature of things, the real way it works, the real good it is designed to serve. Either the strong things in the world are those of self-regard, or they are those of self-forgetting love.

Here is the test of what you mean by faith in Christ. What do you mean by it? Has it a meaning?

Look upon Him and ask yourselves what you mean by believing in such a person. Then you will discover, not only that it has a meaning, but that, if it is not the meaning of all things, you do not believe at all. Is Jesus right in imagining that He reveals the Father, that in Him we really see what God is about, both what kind of good He means to achieve and how He purposes to achieve it?

If Jesus was right, then quite clearly the bulk of our ambitions are wrong and most of our methods of seeking them futile. We have had much rhetoric and many schemes for making the world work better for good. But have we asked ourselves the necessary previous questions—the kind of good they will work for, the kind of people for whom they will work, the condition on which their working is effective? It is vain to plan your journey till you have decided on your goal. Is it possible, in spite of all that appears to the contrary, that this way of God's call to serve His purpose in Christ Jesus, in love to Him which is love to men, is the only way in which the world ever will work together for profit, and that the only secure achievement in life is the highest?

THE SIMPLICITY OF THE GOSPEL

2 CORINTHIANS v. 19. 'God was in Christ, reconciling the world unto himself, not imputing their trespasses unto them.'

To be simple is thought to be easy, and to understand simplicity easier still. But few judgments are more superficial. To rid himself of artificiality and complexity is among man's last and highest achievements.

A French philosopher speaks of life as working simply like an artist drawing a picture with one stroke of his pencil, while our mechanical understanding of it is like a child imitating his line with a multitude of little squares. The skill to make that one adequate stroke, or even the sense for its simple perfection, is in every sphere high and difficult, but in no sphere more than religion. Nor anywhere else does failure impose as burdensome complexity.

Some learned persons even think that religion began with simplicity, and that, if only we could work back to primitive religion, we should recover religion's simple essence. But such traces as we can discover tend to show that the primitive, so far from being simple, was an amazing confusion of complicated beliefs and detailed observances. The great prophetic minds alone have achieved simplicity, and no one has perfectly attained it except the Greatest. He reduces it to good-news of the Father to His children. Nothing could be simpler, yet, for our complex minds, few things are more difficult.

The Apostle's statement in our text is his own understanding of this good-news of Jesus; and it, too, is simple when we rid ourselves of the elaborations which have been woven into it till it has ceased to be a gospel and become a system of theology, a code of divine legislation. To rediscover its simplicity, we must banish from our minds every thought about it except that it is just good-news of God and nothing else. For Paul a ministry of reconciliation was the sun-kissed slopes of Olivet, near and friendly in the pure air; for his interpreters it has too often been the precipices of Sinai, wrapped in a thick cloud of dogma which echoes with the heavy rumbling of controversy. The words which to the Apostle were plain every-day speech have become remote and elaborate and technical. 'God was in Christ' to him meant simply the felt presence of the Father in One who was perfectly His Son; to his interpreters it is a complex and mysterious doctrine of Christ's person. 'Reconciling the world,' which was simply turning men from enemies into friends, is expounded by perplexing controversies about prevenient grace. 'Not imputing trespasses,' which was simply the pardon which restores to fellowship in spite of offences, is turned into difficult and forbidding theories of justification. The result

has been to change the simple gospel that God is
a Father just because there is no limit to His love's
endeavour to restore us to our place as His children,
into a plan of salvation, which stands like a frowning
precipice between us and God.

This gospel of the Father is what the Apostle
says was before the law and in respect of which the
law is only a tutor to prepare us for its liberty.

The law, strange to say, always does follow the
gospel which is meant to replace it. Nothing in
human history is more certain, or more unexpected,
or, at first sight, more inexplicable.

In an actual literal sense Paul himself may not
have realised, the Priestly Law he specially intended
is shown by historical study to have followed the
Prophetic Gospel.

Like the Apostle the prophets too felt themselves
ambassadors on behalf of God to beseech men to be
reconciled to Him. God rose up early to send them.
Nine times over Jeremiah repeats the figure of God
getting up at dawn to toil till dark, like a day-
labourer, at this work of winning His erring children.
And He does it for a people who have turned to Him
their backs and not their faces. In essence that is
the same as Paul's gospel that Christ died while we
were yet sinners to commend to us God's love, or
our Lord's still simpler presentation of God as a
Father who sees his erring son a long way off and
runs and falls on his neck and kisses him, and,
without a single question about the past, overwhelms

him with every token of forgiveness. Every prophet
has that same message. Thus Isaiah says, God
'spreads out His hands all the day to a rebellious
people who walk in a way that is not good, after
their own thoughts, and provoke Him to His face
continually.' Moreover all the prophets were assured
that everything God did in the world confirmed their
message, or, as Paul sums it up, 'all things are of
God who reconciled us to Himself through Jesus
Christ.'

God's message is the same at all times and in
all things, and is not different, but only plainer
and fuller and better authenticated in Jesus Christ.
He is no mere incident contrary to the burden of
the rest of creation and revelation, but is the con-
summation and supreme manifestation of all they
mean.

This gospel simplifies religion to faith in the
Father and the service of love to His children.
God, for the prophets, was not housed in temples
or fed by sacrifices or honoured by solemnities,
but 'looked to him who is poor and of a contrite
spirit and who trembles at His word'—a word
concerned only with doing justly and loving mercy
and walking humbly with our God. But, as never in
the world before or since, the Gospel was simplified
by Jesus. God is the Father whose highest perfection appears in kindness to the unthankful and evil:
and, because He is love, we can serve Him only
through His children and especially by His own

perfection of loving those who hate us. As He left no one outside of God's care and no place without God's presence, there was neither Jew nor Greek nor particular seat of ritual worship. Worship of God who is Spirit required only spirit and truth. God's service was the common life: and traditions of the dead past were set aside as making void God's word in life, and purifications as the wrong way of cleansing life, and regulations as the wrong way of directing life.

Both the prophets and Jesus foresaw that the imposing national religion of their time, with its complicated traditions, elaborate sacrifices and ceremonies and multiform regulations, would perish with the nation and the temple. And their predictions were literally fulfilled, with great gain for a religion of the heart and life.

After the prophets, idolatries passed and God was worshipped as one Lord over all. After Jesus, faith was simply in His God and Father, worship a gathering of the two or three in an attic room, without ritual save a meal of fellowship, and without regulation beyond willingness to be first in service and last in honour.

But now comes the strange part. In spite of the prophets, in a sense because of the prophets, our Lord inherited a religion of enormously complicated traditions of the fathers, ostentatious prayings, ritual sacrifices, elaborate purifications and other meticulously regulated sacred doings, with a disregard for humble, penitent faith and righteous dealing so great that it all seemed in His eyes one vast hypocrisy. Yet this structure, so alien to the intention of the prophets, rested on the prophets and, in particular, on the very conviction that God was in them after a manner special and pre-eminent. A nation, it was thought, endowed with such unique organs of revelation must be God's peculiar people, and the unique and sure message from God they had received through the prophets be elaborately enshrined in tradition, ritual and regulation.

Stranger still, after Jesus, and because of Jesus, the Gospel was turned into a yet vaster and more complicated system of law. The Church replaced the nation with claims which made God even more exclusive; sacraments replaced sacrifices and were even more sacerdotal; a more mysterious traditional belief was imposed by a greater external authority; a more elaborate ritual was made valid by a more exacting priestly succession; regulation penetrated deeper into life by means of a vastly more intrusive system of confession and casuistry.

And, what is more, the yoke was heavier just because of the deeper assurance that God was in Christ without limit or imperfection, that the Spirit was not given by measure unto Him, that in Him was fullness of grace and truth, that He was light and in Him was no darkness at all. A church possessing so absolute an organ of revelation seemed more than ever God's peculiar people, its tradition more necessary for enshrining His teaching, its rites for continuing His influence, its priestly corporation for regulating His service.

As all this structure depended on how God was in Christ, there was added, as a new and more burdensome condition of salvation the acceptance, if not the understanding, of correct views of the precise manner of it. Correct views of His person came to appear God's first requirement, till whosoever would be saved must receive, as revealed mysteries guaranteed by the Church, all the metaphysical subtleties about His person enunciated in the Athanasian Creed.

Why, you may well ask, did this happen? If the Gospel is so simple, why was it so laboriously elaborated into law? What has this abstract omnipotence encased in human form to do with the actual Jesus who taught in parables and spoke of nature and human nature, who rejoiced in spirit and felt forsaken in anguish, who took infants in His arms and blessed them and passed scorching judgment upon teachers and rulers, who lived with our limitations and died facing death with our human darkness and anguish? In this Christ we truly feel the beat of the heart of God, but we can no more feel it in the Christ of the formulas than we can feel our own pulse in an artificial limb. And what has it to do with the gospel of reconciliation? A Father who never ceases to watch and work for His erring children cannot be also an offended

Potentate who will only condone our offences upon strict conditions.

The reason is just the reason of the artificial limb. When the simplicity of life from within fails us, we must do the best we can with the laboured complexity of mechanism from without. Religion has the same function for the soul as limbs for the body, for the soul is active and progressive only as it has something sacred to reverence and obey. Some form of faith, therefore, it must have: and, if it have not one which arises simply from our vision of the truth, the higher our need, the more elaboration will be necessary to supply a substitute from without. As the hand needs a more complex artifice than the foot, a higher gospel needs a more complex law to do its work.

The difference between simplicity and elaboration is a question of order. If you begin with God, you quite simply have the Gospel, just as, if you begin with life, you quite simply have the use of your hand.

We can compare it to rhetoric and eloquence. The order of eloquence is simple and natural; the order of rhetoric is laboured and artificial. Yet inward sincerity alone makes the simple and natural possible; and the hardest labour, without it, only increases the unnaturalness and complexity. Still more the simplicity of the Gospel is like true poetry. Poetry is a right ordering of words, and the right order is the simple order. Yet an inspired imagination alone can achieve that simplicity. Effort, without it, merely achieves the elaborate dexterities of recondite rhymes, startling epigrams and fantasies tricked out in curious and antique words.

The order of the simplicity of the Gospel is the order of our text. God is in Christ to reconcile the world to Himself. Whereupon pardon of sin follows and is one with it. So long as we keep to this order, the absolute presence of God in Christ appears in the impossibility of separating anything Jesus ever said or did from the task of manifesting God's mind to His children. His endurance of the contradiction of sinners against Himself, His bearing of the tribulations which cause us to think that God is against us, especially His Cross, which turns defeat and shame and agony and death into pardon and peace and victory over all mortal trials, commend God's love as above all love because it seeks us while we are yet sinners.

But you may here ask, if the Gospel is thus simple, if it is in essence the Father seeking the return of His erring children, why is it not as easy as it is simple, easy to present and easy to understand? Why should the life of His ambassadors be an unbroken record of bitter opposition and persecution and martyrdom? Why, in particular, should Jesus need to be a man of sorrows and commend God's love specially by a death of shame and agony? And why, above all, when they have endured and all this testimony been borne, is the simple freedom of the

Gospel turned into the complicated slavery of the Law?

The gospel of reconciliation is simple as the prodigal coming to himself and going home and finding pardon showered upon him in every token of love. But it is not simpler. The prodigal must come to himself and go home every step of the way and find there the same Father and the same life he fled from, and discover in them freedom and peace and blessedness. However warm his welcome, this requires nothing less than that he who was dead should be alive again. It is simple as life, simple as love. There are no simpler things in the world, but so far are they from being easy that God alone can be their source: and even He can give them only as in spending His life He manifests His love. To be reconciled to God is to be reconciled to Him in His holiness and all it appoints for us and all it requires of us. God beseeches us to be reconciled to Him, but it is to Him as He is, for in nothing less can we be truly blessed. When God in Christ enables us to make this discovery and to go home to Him just as we are, with our sense of our own unworthiness as the measure of His love, we know that He has no thought in His heart about our trespasses except sorrow for our loss and the offer of all His help to live down their consequences and turn their evil into good.

But this is not concerned with mere emotional regrets on our part and condonation of our offences upon conditions on God's part. It has to do with acceptance of God's purpose in our lives as He appoints them. Therefore, He can appeal to us only through those who have accepted it amid life's hardest trials and conflicts; and His only perfect appeal is through Him who bore all our griefs and carried all our sorrows and turned shame and agony and death into victory and pardon and the love from which nothing can separate us.

But when we fail to follow the way of love which begins with God seeking to reconcile us to Himself, we must try the way of law which begins with our trespasses, as though the prodigal had not first said, I will arise and go to my father, willing to be with him even as a hired servant, but had proceeded to inquire on what terms the past would be overlooked or condoned.

It is only a question of order, but it is like the order of our work and our wage. Our work put first, the earning of our wage is one with the doing of it; our wage put first, our work is a distinct and painful condition unfortunately attached to it. The right order is simple, but cannot be followed with less than the spirit of duty. So the right order of reconciliation we can follow only by the faith which works by love.

Failing this, we must take the legal order and start with the conditions upon which God is willing to be reconciled. Forthwith God is no more for us in Christ as the simple persuasive incarnation of

His love to the unthankful and evil, which makes all things work together to reconcile them to His mind and purpose. On the contrary, Christ's work must be explained in some way as the condition upon which God pardons. It is a condition to satisfy God's righteousness, and no longer an appeal which has no condition except returning to a righteous God. It is to satisfy a just Ruler and permit Him to condone our offences, whereas the only consequence of sin Jesus ever greatly concerned Himself with was its power to alienate us from our Father, and the only pardon which ever satisfied Him was restoration to God's friendship and peace. To desire any other pardon only shows that we are still following our way of blessedness, and not Christ's. We are seeking happiness by freedom from evil, whereas true reconciliation to God is a recognition that no evil is to be shunned which brings us to Him and no pleasure or possession reckoned good which keeps us from Him. The riotous abundance which detains us in the far country is loss, and the swine-keeping and the husks are gain which bring us home.

Failing this change in our thought of blessedness, we must betake ourselves to moral subtleties about imputation, puzzling doctrines about justification, burdensome sacerdotal appliances to communicate grace, and cramping, regulated obediences to fulfil God's requirements. Christ's yoke is no more easy and His burden no more light, but He becomes a further load of traditional dogma upon our faith and of ecclesiastical authority upon our lives.

Only when we discover that our blessedness is in God as He is and as He deals with us, can we find Christ simply the heart of the Father commending His love to us, overwhelming us with every token of forgiveness and every proof of complete restoration to our place as His children.

Yet simple as it is, it is not easy, else there had been no Cross. Its demands are not small. The heaviest requirements of law are finite; every requirement of love is infinite and leaves us, after we have done our utmost, still unprofitable. But it makes no demand without its own succour. Nor does it ask obedience except in its own freedom. If the yoke is not easy and light, as lightness and ease are reckoned in the far country, it is so by the strength and joy which come from knowing that all things are of God who reconciles us to Himself through Jesus Christ, with whom we are heirs of God who makes all things ours both for the highest uses of time and the surest hopes of eternity, and whose blessing makes rich and adds no sorrow.

XI

GOD'S FAILURES

LUKE xvii. 17–18. 'And Jesus answering said, "Were not the ten cleansed? but where are the nine? Were there none found that returned to give glory to God, save this stranger?"'

THE strangest feature of this incident is our Lord's unprotesting acceptance of the situation. One alone returns, while nine go their ungrateful way: and He leaves it there. He works no miracle on their diseased souls, such as He had done on their diseased bodies; and He does not even remonstrate or appeal, though by either way He could have produced at least correctness of behaviour.

And, as Jesus did, God manifestly does every day. He sets right no visible defection by outward correction, and works no change of heart or direction of will by miraculous power. Day by day He makes His appeal of goodness; and when that fails, He accepts failure. This is the problem we have to consider.

1. GOD FAILS WITH SIGNAL MERCIES CHIEFLY BECAUSE HE FAILS WITH THE COMMON EXPERIENCES

Even as an isolated lapse of an otherwise grateful humanity, this incident would be a painful revelation of the possibilities of human nature; and only a cynic, you might imagine, would regard the action of these nine Jews as typical of mankind. Yet this ingratitude was no unique experience for Jesus, and He does not seem to have thought it exceptional in God's experience of His children.

Personal application to ourselves we should all resent. We may have been blind to many blessings when they were veiled by familiarity or by slow realisation, but is it conceivable that a deliverance, impressive by its greatness, its suddenness, its transforming effect, should not stir our hearts to their depths? Think of the pit of misery from which these lepers had been drawn. Think of days of hideous suspense slowly changing to ghastly certainty, of the bright canopy of heaven turned into the black shroud of dead hopes, of acquaintances passing with averted faces, of intimate friends arresting themselves with a shudder, of homes shadowed at once by horror at their presence and fear of a separation more awful than the grave. Then realise the desolate waste, the bare shelter, the fellowship only of companions in misery. Broken, suffering, loathsome, they had cried for help, like Jonah, 'out of the belly of hell.' When this appalling misery passed suddenly, like an awful nightmare with the dawn, surely, like Jonah also, they would sacrifice unto God with the voice of thanksgiving and pay what they had vowed, knowing that their salvation was of the Lord.

But while you may reasonably be confident of

showing better manners, can you be equally sure of feeling deeper gratitude? Before you can be quite sure that in your inmost heart it would be otherwise with you, try to imagine the actual thoughts of these Jews. As disfigurement fell from their faces, and renewed vigour surged through their veins, and hope soared aloft from its grave, they saw themselves once again amid all the interests, activities and ambitions of their old lives. But, at the thought of home, consider how it would flash upon them that their old life might not be waiting. Were they not dead men out of mind, their acquaintances forgetful, their friends consoled, their offices assigned to others, their heirs secure in their possessions? Then the pit from which they had been drawn seemed ready to swallow them back into darkness and oblivion. At the thought everything would be blotted from their minds except the need of haste to claim their place in the land of the living before time had wholly filled it with the interests of others.

If self-regard rightly hold the place they gave it, they had reason for attending to business first and gratitude afterwards. Are you sure that it is the place you think wrong? Yet this it was that proved their action no mere lapse of a moment, but the outcome of lives habitually self-centred. They failed to observe the comet because they had ceased to regard the stars, though the stars, more than the comet, should be the spring of unutterable thoughts.

The offence is thereby made greater, but is it not

also brought closer to each of us? A failure which springs from blindness to life's constant possibilities, can be escaped only by those for whom life is no routine pursuit of self-regarding ends.

Nor need we suppose a very poor type of self-regard, or thoughts mean and wholly material. Self-regarding possession is not necessarily selfish possession. With restoration to life and hope the love of wife and child would surge up in their hearts anew, and an immense desire would flame before each one to witness the joy in his home as he came back to it from his 'charnel cave.' And, around their own households, they would see the homesteads of their neighbours and the cheerful, bustling, friendly world in which they might once again play their part.

To the kindly self many good and beautiful things belong. It is a pleasant thing to behold the sun and the love in human eyes which shines in its light, and there are things which spring under its warmth, which are blessed to give as well as to receive. Yet it may still be merely a roundabout way of going inward from the gift to the receiver and not a direct way of going outward to the Giver, thus making God's own goodness the supreme reason for forgetting Him.

Nor will it be otherwise in great deliverances, unless there is habitual returning to give glory to God for the common mercies, not as a mere matter of custom or form, but as the impulse of heartfelt gratitude. What are the usual thoughts of men who have been raised from mortal sickness, or have escaped destruction by a hair's breadth? How often are their real thanks to their constitutions, or their fortunes or their skill, and their immediate thoughts concerned with recovering their place in the world they had seemed so near to losing!

Considering how constantly you take your privileges to be merely your due, can you be sure that any deliverance would seem to you more than the mere restoration of what is yours in your own right? Is not health better than recovery, and the unbroken enjoyment of life's blessings better than their restoration? Think of the abiding wonder of earth and air, and 'the human face divine,' and home and kindred, and the joy of living and thought and aspiration, and of the greatest marvel of all, that for us they are common and continuous. If, for this, you have never returned to give glory to God, is it not a fond illusion to suppose that any deliverance in the world would be signal enough to stir your gratitude, or any experience poignant enough to 'stab your spirits broad awake'?

God's first failure was not with His chastening, but with the blessings it had withdrawn. Feeding swine and eating husks, by which the prodigal came to himself, was a pastime compared with the experience of these Jews, yet they came to themselves only in the self-centred sense which leads to no Father. Their haste to turn their backs on their misery shows with what thoughts they had endured it. Were they not good citizens, honest in business, kindly at home, regular at worship, generous to good objects, blameless before men and deserving well of God? How unjust that this fell disease should shut them up in a more terrible imprisonment than could be inflicted on the worst criminal! Their hearts were broken, but not humbled; their eyes were blinded by tears of resentment, but not purged by dews of sorrow; they had been scourged, but, in no sense, chastened.

Having got nothing save bitterness out of trial, they got nothing save self-satisfaction out of deliverance. It was God, not they, who had seen the error of His ways; and they were merely at length restored to their due.

Only as we are exercised by affliction, and not as we resent it, can deliverance work gratitude. Otherwise, we know neither how to sorrow nor how to rejoice. Our feeling is like the leprous skin, which does not rightly respond to any influence from without, but ever returns in upon itself, to shut us up more closely in our self-regard. The heart either goes out to God by our experience and is blessed by all of it in God's varied world, by the cold of winter as well as the warmth of summer, by battling with the storm as well as by basking in the sunshine, or it returns upon itself and pines in the darkened prison-house of its own soul: and God can provide neither discipline nor deliverance which would call us forth to freedom under His open heavens.

If what you do in small things is the index of what you would do in great, might not you too emerge out of torture and despair only to think of yourselves as deprived of your rights, and to take your return to your former state as merely tardy justice to your merits? And, as many a sorrowful example teaches us, God accepts this verdict of the heart of man, and apparently leaves the matter as it decides.

2. GOD FAILS WITH LIFE BECAUSE HE FAILS WITH THE COMMON RELIGION

All the nine who went away were Jews; the only one who returned was a Samaritan.

The position of the Jew in religion was truly privileged. Though Paul was the Apostle of the Gentiles, he thought that the Jews had the advantage every way, and more especially because to them were committed the oracles of God; and our Lord, even while maintaining that God is a spirit to be worshipped by all alike in spirit and in truth, regarded salvation as of the Jews.

How great the advantage was appears when we remember that the Scripture of the Samaritans was confined to the Pentateuch, the most ceremonial and least spiritual part of the Old Testament, and that even this very restricted portion of Holy Writ had been received by them more in superstition

than in piety. Had this Samaritan's religion con-
sisted in mere formal obedience and respect for
ritual observance to secure temporal prosperity, we
need not have thought it strange, seeing how he
did not know the prophets and psalmists, who
taught that God would have mercy and not sacrifice,
and that God's thoughts for His children were as
high above their thoughts for themselves as the
heavens are above the earth, and that the servant
of the Lord has to win his victories by being a man
of sorrows and acquainted with grief. Or, if he
knew anything of such teaching, it could only have
been through his Jewish associates. There is such a
thing as preaching successfully to others and being
ourselves cast-away. The sun's rays which warm the
earth travel through cold spaces, the stream which
fertilises the plain springs from the barren rock, and
the truth which makes alive may pass through dead
souls.

What sent these Jews off so hastily was the command to show themselves to the priest. No small
part of their eagerness was the desire to return to
their religious privileges. They were, after the same
fashion as the Athenians, very religious. Of nothing
in their old life were they prouder than their religious
doings; and we can imagine them often beguiling
the weary hours by speaking of them, as the Samaritan sat silently attentive. Nor need we suppose
that, in their affliction, their religion had been no
consolation. But it had not enabled them to under-

stand how health could be loss without God and even leprosy gain with God. There is only one religious discovery of value. It is not that God is behind all events, for that may only make them more terrible and strange. It is that God is in all events, even when they are not of His causing but of our sins, and that, by His purpose and succour, they may all be turned to good. These Jews had great means in their common religion for making this discovery. Recall how, directly and indirectly, our Lord constantly used the Old Testament, and how, without it, even Peter and Paul could not have understood Him. A high revelation through those who have found God in their experiences is a supreme gain for finding Him in our own; and a mind full of ignorance and superstition is a great hindrance. But, when we turn religion from its true purpose, missing the spirit and venerating the letter, the highest religion may be the greatest obstacle.

As soon as these Jews heard the injunction, 'Go show yourselves to the priest,' all their pride of religious caste blazed up in them. They did exactly what Jesus told them to do. In spite of their hurry to go home, they would go round about by the road of ceremonial purification. They obeyed to the letter, but it was the letter which the prompting of true gratitude made the Samaritan disregard. Their hearts swelled with pride when reminded that they were Abraham's seed and might once more claim their heritage as members of God's peculiar people.

This blotted out for them all thought that they were His sinful children, to whom He had so recently shown signal mercy.

In contrast, the Samaritan, ignoring the letter, found that a very imperfect religion opened the heavens and made his face radiant with joy and gratitude. It also brought him back to Jesus Himself, to find in Him the full revelation of the Father which would turn for him henceforth all life's experiences into a manifestation of a love which would enable him in all things to give thanks.

Yet, even with this supreme manifestation of Himself, God may fail. Jesus Himself can be turned from being a vision to our own insight, an inspiration to our own devotion, an appeal to our own hearts, a victory for our own lives, into the supreme sanction of formulas, the supreme enslavement to institutions, the supreme imposition of rules and ceremonies. Men still can say 'Lord, Lord' and do outwardly all kinds of things in His name, and only the more fail to reach the reality of all He means, using the formulas about His person and the forms of His service, not as the life and the truth which are the way to the Father, but as the observances and the traditions which make His word of none effect, till, above every other cause, they stand between the soul and the living God, and cloud the sense that all things are from Him and unto Him.

3. God fails with religion because He fails with the common intercourse

While the Jews obeyed the letter, the Samaritan disobeyed, being prompted of his own heart and led by the spirit which makes alive.

As he turned, they could not fail to see him; and, as he shouted his praise, they could not fail to hear him. But by the name of stranger Jesus called him; and He did not use the word carelessly. From the moment they were healed, the one thought of his companions was how he might henceforth be to them an utter stranger, how most easily they could turn their backs on him for good. And that shows what thoughts had been associated with him all the time. Their adversity had compelled them to put up with this alien bed-fellow. Perhaps their very abruptness in cutting his acquaintance showed that he had won their regard and even some measure of affection, and that in his company they had almost ceased to be Jews and become men. But, how would it stand with them, they reflected, should their fellow-worshippers learn of this contamination? Here was a providential way of escape, without harsh explanation or painful parting. The Samaritan had turned back, and the whole affair could be settled simply by hurrying on.

Their very kindliness exposed them the more to the temptation. But it was a kindliness which returned to everything bitter, narrow, sectarian, formal. Peace

and charity and sincerity they left behind in leaving
Jesus. And—what was worse—it would have been
vain to stay, because they had also turned away from
all the deep things of the heart of humanity to which
Jesus appealed.

In fleeing from this alien, they fled from their old
life and all its lessons. The deepest lesson of what
God meant for them, not as Jews but as men, they
had perhaps dimly understood in his company. As
they fled from him, all discovery of the deep things
of the soul of man, and all possibility of ever discerning that it was good for them to have been afflicted,
vanished.

Suppose instead that he had become their first
care, that no prejudice could have come between
them any more and no change have divided their
fellowship, and we cannot imagine them failing to
see the Father in their Deliverer. But their haste
to be rid of the Samaritan showed that he was
associated in their minds only with sad and bitter
thoughts, thoughts to be escaped, not cherished. He
spoke to them of days when they were aggrieved
but not penitent, of days when their outward confession of God did not ward from their hearts the
bitterest rebellion against His appointment for their
lives, of days to be forgotten and not valued. In
the last resort, God failed with all He appointed
both of distress and of deliverance, because He failed
with the ministry of this Samaritan.

Your Samaritan, too, is always the person from

whom your instinct of superiority would make you flee; and your treatment of him, above all else, decides how God can reveal Himself to your soul as the living God, and what He can make out of you by means of your fellows.

Christ's own supreme test is how you deal with one of the little ones. The little one is ignorant, but ever seeks light; lags behind, but never ceases to aspire; has many moral falls, but ever stumbles forward; gropes often in the dark, but ever seeks the light; is not a shining example, but is wholly sincere; often lacks wisdom, but the instinct of his affection is always right. As you treat him, you show whether God has been able to teach you that there is nothing here with any of us save God's erring child and His unwavering love.

Yet, if God is not to fail with you, you must go still farther. Your Samaritan may be a child, hungry and neglected, till it has lost all the charm of childhood, or a foolish youth dangerously playing with temptation, till he exhausts your patience, or an inefficient person searching fruitlessly for a place in a crowded world, till by his vacillation he forfeits your esteem, or a man who has little courage because he has little character. He may even be one whom intemperance and lust have degraded and to whom thoughts of good come only as fitful gleams of light on a winter day. Yet by him, most of all, you may find the Father, and by the Father all the true uses of life.

Books, even the Bible, and forms of worship,

even the highest, and organised societies, even the
purest, are not religion, but only aids to religion,
aids, moreover, do not forget, which you can turn
into hindrances. To receive the Lord, you must
receive those He sends; to visit Him, you must
visit His sick and captive disciples. Above all, to
know freely His mind and what it reveals of the
perfection of our Father in Heaven, you must deal
as He does, not only with the imperfect, but with
the unthankful and evil.

In the company of your Samaritan you will learn
the reason of God's failures, and know that it is
of reverence for His children, and not of weakness.
Whether you find sincerity and responsiveness and
humility and aspiration and readiness to give the
glory to God, or continuance in error and evil in a
way to cause you to marvel at God's forbearance,
you will be in the way of understanding the thoughts
of God's heart towards the children He has made
in His own image, and you will be enabled to find
all life the appeal of His love.

If love is, in this way, moral reverence for those
God has made in His own image, a confident and
dogmatic assurance of universal salvation ceases to
be its undeniable outcome, and for all God's working
of the willing and the doing in us, our salvation
must be wrought out with fear and trembling.

In one sense God leaves it there, in the sense that
He cannot alter His ways of appeal. But He would
not be a Father at all, if this meant that His purpose

of good could end. Jesus constantly accepted the verdict of man's ingratitude, yet He never was in any way discouraged by it. He went on as before, revealing the Father, pleading by word and deed, giving Himself unreservedly for those who rejected Him, living for them, and, in the end, dying for them.

That death, commending God's love to us while we were yet sinners, is the highest manifestation of the heart of God this world affords; and we may not rashly assume that there could be anything even in another life which could set it in a clearer light. No more in another life than in this can any display of power take its place to turn our hearts truly to God. The supremest privileges of another world, even as of this, might be used only to feed self-esteem, and so to shut us off from our brethren, and so from our Father.

Yet we do not readily admit the limits of love's resources, even as we poor finite creatures may employ them. Did we say, as sometimes it has been said, that in the Cross of Christ God has done all He can do, and, love having justified itself, justice must take its course, should we be thinking adequately of the heart of God? In which way would the Cross be the highest manifestation of the Father? Would it be as the last demonstration of mercy before abandoning the sinner? Or would it not rather be as the supreme assurance that His mercy never could be exhausted? If the Cross is love's highest evidence, how can it be love's outermost boundary? Is it not rather a declaration that love is without bounds?

A benefit unacknowledged is so often turned to bitterness that we can easily imagine the nine among those who shouted loudest 'Crucify Him! Crucify Him!' to the Master. But what if we were to think of them as among those who on the Day of Pentecost were pricked in their hearts, and who cried out to the disciples as they had never done to the Master, "Brethren what shall we do?" and all because the appeal, which, though it had made them bitter, they never could live down, was just the memory of their benefactor sorrowful but un-remonstrating! And when shall we say that possibility is exhausted?

At all events this is the only kind of success with which God will be satisfied. On it He stakes everything, and, till He wins it, He is content to accept failure without any thought of replacing it by any form of compelling assent.

XII

THE PEACEMAKER AND THE PEACEABLE

MATTHEW v. 9. 'Blessed are the peacemakers: for they shall be called sons of God.'

On one occasion I was asked to preside at a meeting of prayer for all the churches. There was a printed programme of the things we were to pray for. The first sentence which caught my eye was: "That ministers should cease to preach upon problems." That petition, I fancy, would find an echo in many hearts.

If you have come to the house of God primarily to worship, the intrusion of problems, whether of thought or of action, will be apt to chill and repel. Why should they be intruded upon you? Should not the sanctuary be above all else a place of calm? May we not say for a little to the struggle of life: Stay here outside, while I go yonder and worship? For one short hour may we not turn aside from the fevered hurry of life to stand in the changeless presence of God? If, at such a moment, anyone venture to speak to us, may we not ask that he dwell only on the pardon of sin, the grace which succours our weak will, the love which turns affliction to blessing, the might which makes all things work together for our good? May we never leave outside the turmoil of the world, and, by looking for a little at the glory of God in the face of Jesus Christ, endeavour to catch a glimpse of the city which has foundations, not in the problems of the present, but in the eternal verities?

If, on such good grounds, the preacher can speak comfortably to Jerusalem and say unto her, Thy God reigneth, and give her the oil of joy for mourning, why, in the name of common sense as well as of religion, should he ever preach politically or socially? Why, when he can lay his hand in healing upon bruised and wearied souls, should he even preach morally? Why is he not content simply to preach a gospel which lays us at rest in the great calm which is at the heart of life and which is God?

All this seems utterly convincing: yet there is another way of looking at the matter which is also convincing.

What is the religion worth which shuts itself in with thick walls and will not allow the light of heaven to enter except through stained-glass and which drowns the world's clamour and wail with the roll of organs? Who are you to be happy in the central calm like a pagan god, while without is injustice, naked force, cruel greed, rags, hunger, vice and crime? Can true religion, and above all the religion of Jesus Christ, be heedless of any task of public justice and righteousness, or of private compassion and fair dealing?

How with the crying actualities of evil and pain at our doors, racking real flesh and blood, should a preacher waste his time at all on the generalities of pardon and grace and eternal life? Is he not plainly shirking the demands of Christ, refusing to follow those who in His name resisted unto blood striving against sin, and, while professing to reverence the word of the Cross, in reality making it of none effect?

Both views seem alike convincing, yet are they not in flat contradiction? Nor is it a mere matter of argument. Do they not represent moods which in most of us are in unceasing conflict? Is there any possible way except to live for the most part in face of the present distress and to turn from it occasionally to the eternal calm?

But this is the very secret of the peacemaker that in him the eternal calm and the present distress are not alien and opposite and irreconcilable. Like God Himself all evil finds in him an implacable foe; and like God also the mightiest weapon of his warfare is a peace evil cannot assail.

For this resemblance to God he is called a son of God. In these beatitudes each virtue has its own appropriate blessing. Those who hunger and thirst after righteousness are filled; those who mourn are comforted; the pure in heart see God. With like appropriateness the peacemakers are called sons of

God. Doing God's work in God's way, they hear through all life's turmoil the Spirit of God crying in their hearts, 'Abba, Father,' so that they are as calm as they are intrepid, as full of life's realities in the sanctuary as of the spirit of adoration and worship in the day of battle.

But it is the peacemaker who has this secret and is a son of God, not the peaceable. The peaceable is only a maker of ease, a very different matter from a maker of peace. A maker of ease God most certainly is not. In life, as it comes from Him, slackness means defeat, and defeat means death. He appoints suffering and He permits sin. The reasons may be mysterious, but about the practical issue there is no dubiety. It means that God will have His children 'mount and that hardly to eternal life,' coming home to Him with the crown of victory on their heads and the light of battle in their eyes. Our leader is the Captain of our Salvation whom the hypocrisies of this world mocked and scourged and crucified and laid in a tomb. The key to it all is the Cross, the cross of utter obedience, of absolute loyalty, of implacable conflict with evil, of final victory over sin.

You can see who the peacemakers are by the account of what happens to them. They are persecuted for righteousness sake and are reviled and have all manner of evil said against them falsely. This happens to them precisely because they are not the peaceable, because they do not accept things as they are, letting sleeping dogs lie, leaving well alone, and generally obeying the prudent maxims which ensure a quiet life. On the contrary, like all true guardians of the peace, they are resolute, uncompromising fighters against every disturbing, disruptive force. And that means they are foes of all evil, for all evil is disturbing and disruptive. You cannot, as the prophet said long ago, make an agreement with hell to be at peace with it: and without a clear mind on that point there is no being a peacemaker.

The peaceable never admits that impossibility. Not discerning that the disruptive force in all sin is selfishness, of which love of ease is one of the worst manifestations, he sits down in the world, like a mother who hopes for quiet by trying to ignore the Babel of which her own slackness is the source. Like the ancient kings of Israel, he prays that the reckoning shall not be in his time, however much his time may augment the score. He would run the risk of a malaria in the future, rather than disturb the cesspools in the present.

But the true peacemaker is precisely the person who has no toleration for the world's cesspools, who knows that an undisturbed injustice, an undisturbed wrong of any kind is the place where the pestilence necessarily breeds. Nor does he deal with it timidly or with feeble tools. He is no peacemaker who has no iron in his blood, no hot word of indignation at fitting times on his tongue, who is not ready, when occasion calls, to be a follower of Him who could flash forth, 'Woe unto you Scribes and Pharisees, hypocrites,' and who spoke with appalling concreteness of the wrong combination of work and worship—devouring widows' houses and making long prayers.

The merely peaceable, on the other hand, has one supreme device for seeking peace. It is to put expediency for principle. The adept at that exchange is frequently described as a safe man. Nor in any sphere is he thought safer than in the Church. History rather confirms the judgment that he is the most dangerous man in it, yet to this day men have not ceased to believe in him, with his average opinions, which are not opinions at all, his dull, formal decisions, which are not decisions at all, his course shaped only to float with the current, which is not a course at all.

Nor is it only in the Church that such a man is dangerous. Under his shelter all abuses tend to gather, all the poisonous low vapours which only the lightning and the hurricane can purge away. The evil which corrupts the world is not fostered mainly by bad men, but by ease-loving men who will never take their stand upon principle and dare the consequences. Evil only prospers so abundantly because it can count so securely on such compliance and cowardice.

A wholly perverted idea of Christian meekness takes it to be acceptance of things as they are as the will of God. Serious men, who have no wish to travesty Christianity, believe that it is the Christian temper to sit down and fold our hands while disease festers in the dark, and injustice makes use of the civil powers, and wars are stirred up from oppression or greed of gold. They have even come to think that this is what Christ meant by being a peacemaker.

But, if we have given cause for the misunderstanding, He never did. He who is supremely the Son of God was a peacemaker of a different order. In that sense of peace, He brought not peace but a sword. He troubled the State and rent the Church; He created a whirlwind of infinite desire and unsatisfied longing in the heart of man; before Him the measured pagan calm forsook man's brow. Those who went out in His name turned the world upside down: and no one has ever truly learned His spirit to this day who is not a disturber of conventions and formalities and agreements with hell to be at peace with it. 'My peace,' said the Master, 'I give unto you': yet it was certainly not as the world gives it, but with Gethsemane and Calvary in it, with sin crushed and love victorious, and God's will done on a hostile earth as in a favouring heaven. And His followers are those who resist unto blood striving against sin: and they and they alone are the true peacemakers.

Yet, though every peacemaker is a fighter, every fighter is not a peacemaker. To be a peacemaker we must fight in peace as well as for it.

There was a fisherman whose face used to haunt me when I was a boy. Afterwards I learned the secret of it. Even when you see peace, in most faces it only shimmers on the surface, like a sunbeam across rippling water, but on his face it was like the reflection of the azure heavens from placid ocean depths. Yet, it was said that absolute calm was only seen on it when the cloud-rack and the spin-drift began to meet. Nor did anyone doubt that the source of it was a more intense realisation at such a time of the God who holds the waters in the hollow of His hand.

There was a strange, reverent sense, even among his not very religious fellow-craftsmen, that nothing else brought him through a storm which overtook him one day out on the Atlantic in an open boat, which was so sudden and violent that his companion was paralysed by fear, leaving as his only helper his son, a boy so young and inexperienced as scarce to know one rope from another. They felt that he had a power to think and act which no mere skill or courage could give, and that if, in spite of it, the worst had happened, it would still have enabled him to go down with his last thought, not of fear, but of saving others.

Such is your true peacemaker, your really strong fighter amid the welter of human ill, your utterly reliable steersman in the storm of life. The state he guides from her council chamber to her humblest cottage is secure. Nor, in face of every uncertainty and possibility, is there any equipment for the humblest responsibility except the calm which reflects in placid faith the infinite heaven above.

Yet it is not given to all, or to anyone at all times, to have a peace which works by knowledge and foresight and skill. In that boat there was also another kind of peace, without which it would never have reached harbour. While the other man was helpless, because he looked only on the tumult of the sea, the child was able to do what was needed, because he was conscious of little save his father's face, from which he read what was required of him and received the quietness and strength necessary for the doing of it. Why it was done he might not know; that it must be done he accepted from a wisdom beyond his own. Thus he too was an efficient worker for deliverance, being also a peacemaker because he was himself at peace.

Such childlike peace may seem weaker and less discerning, but what else is equal to all emergencies? When troubles 'roar like the roaring of the sea, and the light is darkened in the heavens, and counsel perishes from the wise,' the only wisdom available is to stand in our place and look up into the face of the Great Steersman of the world's barque, who alone knows its course and its port, and try to catch, through the mists and the darkness, His directions, and to carry them out, from moment to moment, in the task which lies nearest.

And, if life is, as we have seen, more like a battle

than a sea-faring, more of a fight for victory than a flight for safety, a battle, too, in the universal warfare between light and darkness, evil and good, the peace of the poor in spirit, who know that their only guidance is of God, is still more exclusively and continuously an abiding need when the battle is with confused noise of the warriors and the earth is filled with 'blood and fire and pillars of smoke.' Who can go forward resolute and secure, except as he realises that he is only a private in the great conflict the large issues of which he cannot know, appointed to his place by a General who will not forget him even on the lonely outpost or the midnight skirmish, whose directions turn the immediate task into the service of an eternal purpose?

Only when we thus fight with God to guide and sustain, can we fight in love, without which no fighting is peace-making. Love must often fight, and sometimes in anger, but it must never cease to be love. All its warfare is to save not to destroy, to pardon not to avenge, to establish mercy and not mere justice. Even indignation must not only be akin to pity, but be ever ready to change into it; and it must be purged of violence by knowing that 'the name of the wicked shall rot,' that sin, being folly and weakness, and not merely aggressiveness and wrong, is to be pitied and not to be feared. Above the worst tumult it must hear a calm voice saying, 'The Lord is in His holy temple, let all the earth keep silence before Him.'

The soul of religion, therefore, is still worship. A religion which is mere use of the moral scourge, angry and hortatory and primarily concerned with having things done, is missing its power as well as its peace. It creates nervous excitement not strength, foolish interference not calm and efficient wisdom. And it is sure to overlook the chief need, which is just the spirit of love itself, the only thing in the end that can be truly just as well as merciful.

A distinguished statesman has told us that the first business of the Church is to keep statesmen alive to the claims of justice and want, and so to forward reform, remove oppression, remedy poverty and ill-health, and gradually eliminate all human ills. For the church in the atmosphere of which enthusiasm for that aim cannot flourish little is to be said. But the church which does not derive this from a higher inspiration has also missed its vocation. Even for the economic battle we have to do more than fight self-interest with other self-interests; and for peace in the world we have to do more than oppose violence to violence. No device has ever yet been discovered whereby in such battles the weakest do not go to the wall. To have any hope of success we have to put the whole matter on the level of reverence for man as man, justice as in God's sight, pity as between fellow-travellers from time to eternity, compassion as from those who need compassion, responsibility for talents, wealth, opportunity, privilege, as gifts from God wherewith to serve.

This means that no one can be a true peacemaker who has not God's peace, which is just God's love, in his heart. He must be a man, the current of whose life runs too deep for earthly strife to ruffle, because it springs from the perennial fountain of pardon, grace and eternal life. If that be the source of his power, the first need of his life will be a fellowship in worship, a fellowship where he will unite with all his brethren, master and workman, friend and foe, to look up into the face of their common Father. Especially it will be a fellowship where he will see God's face in the face that was more marred by conflict with the world's sin and sorrow than any man's, and yet in which is seen, as nowhere else, the glory of God.

As we stand before the Cross, seeing the nails and the scourge and the crown of thorns, but hearing only pitying forgiveness and the assurance of a finished work, pardon and peace should settle on our faces also and the clamour of evil should be silenced and the paltriness and uncertainty of our own endeavour be taken up into the Divine sacrifice and service for men.

That must be the inner sanctuary of our worship, and there only can we find the perennial source of our peace. But it is also a sanctuary where no demand, however clamorous, however conflicting, can be inconsistent with our worship. No worship, however rapt and serene, should be inconsistent with any conflict, any duty, any problem, any distress.

Except we never divorce the things of conflict and of calm which God has joined, we cannot be the peacemakers, who are called the children of God because, like Him, they are opponents of every evil, yet abide in the calm of the unchanging vision of good, because they have at once the light of temporal battle in their eyes and the peace of eternity in their hearts. We shall thus abide possessed of the true weapons of our warfare, which are forbearance, pity, justice; and we shall ever employ them in the power of the spirit of love, and be peacemakers who are ourselves at peace.

XIII

THE MAN AND THE OCCASION

1 Samuel x. 7. 'And let it be, when these signs are come unto thee, that thou do as occasion serve thee; for God is with thee.'

'Saul went forth to seek his father's asses and found a kingdom' sounds like a transformation in fairy land, but Saul himself was far from certain that the asses were profitably exchanged.

Unwillingness to rule, Plato says, is the first qualification for a ruler. In that respect Saul was well equipped: and for the good reason of thinking the honour small and the responsibility great. But this qualification, however convincing to others, can hardly impress its possessor, if, like Saul, he perceive no other fitness either in himself or the position of his family.

Nor could anyone have seen much more than he saw himself. A young farmer, more concerned about his strayed asses than his oppressed country, and with a notion of religion as a device for discovering their whereabouts, was not a very promising agent to stir a patriotic and religious revolt in a people sunk in abject submission to a vigilant and powerful oppressor. Nay, any man ever born might have shrunk from the task proposed to Saul of collecting an army under the eyes of so wary a foe and arming it and feeding it in a country carefully searched for weapons and foraged for provender.

What wonder, then, if the consecrating oil made Saul feel rather like a victim anointed for sacrifice than a royal person, while the shadowy crown made his head feel loose upon his shoulders, as though a breath would sigh it off.

Nor did Samuel himself, who launched him on this perilous voyage, think very differently of the man Saul was. What he anointed was the man Saul would become when God's signs had come unto him. This becoming another man was the Prophet's sole programme for a national hero and deliverer: and other plan or caution or hint of method he offered none. Become the right man, then take the first current at its flood. 'Thou shalt do as occasion serves, for God is with thee': and that was all.

These signs, at first sight, seem purely accidental and arbitrary, with no natural fitness either to direct to a right use of occasion or to assure God being with him. But a closer view will show that they are the sole authentic signs of an eye that sees and a heart that ventures.

As his first sign, Saul would meet two men by Rachel's sepulchre at Zelzah on the border of Benjamin, who would tell him that the asses he went to seek were found, but that his father had left off caring for the asses and was saying, 'What shall I do for my son?'

This was all familiar enough. Many a time no

doubt before he had visited the sepulchre of Rachel, the ancestress of his tribe. Nor could it have been information that his father, however keen a husbandman, loved his son above his cattle. But life's great signs are seldom new. What transforms men is a new discovery of the meaning of the old, of the elemental and eternal in the familiar and commonplace.

Jacob had passed over Jordan with nothing but his staff. He came back over it with oxen and asses, flocks and man-servants and maid-servants, and all a country-bred mind could imagine of opulence. Kish, Saul's father, was, in his own degree, another Jacob. And for Saul a similar career stood for all the world could offer of dazzling success. But ere this simple way-side grave and the vision of his father, wandering, like Jacob, among his substance, bereaved and desolate, had finished speaking to him, he saw, with the fresh wonder of new discovery, how much more life depends for its value on what we love than on what we have. Here in love of husband and wife, father and son, was a good, precious beyond flocks and herds and even kingdoms, nay even life itself.

Was not that an authentic sign for a national deliverer, seeing how it revealed to him the true cause he was to champion, and manifested its worthiness to command all hazard and sacrifice? While his own safety was surely as important as the security of his neighbour's sheep-cotes, the inviolable sacredness of his neighbour's hearth was another matter. Could Saul make every home in Israel a peaceful sanctuary for the love of husband and wife, parent and child, even if the end of his enterprise should be a way-side grave where hands that loved him laid him, as Jacob had laid Rachel, his life would have been spent to purpose, and death be a small price for so high a gain.

A serious view of life, Matthew Arnold says, is the first mark of a true poet. Many failings he may have, but a frivolous estimate of man by his worldly trappings must not be one. Reality must lie for him in the experiences of the heart, and they, and not man's estate, must absorb his interest. The story of Rachel and the grave at Zelzah is the very stuff of poetry: the prosperity of Jacob, through overreaching his astute father-in-law, will sing itself into no song. Similarly, without something of this poetic gift in his soul, interpreting life by the authentic sign of love for his fellows simply as men and women, no man can discover God's true inheritance, or have any call to be a captain over it. He must not see men merely in the mass, as so many hands for work or units for armies, or distinguish them only by position and wealth, but he must see each with his own strange, eventful story of love's young dream and manhood's loyalties, of fellowship and loneliness, of hope and despair, of success and failure, and the mystery of death must shed dignity for him even on the commonest. The man who misses this sign, though he attain all else that place and fortune can provide, remains in God's real kingdom a mere hewer of wood and drawer of water.

As the first sign showed Saul his true task, the second instructed him as to the means for achieving it.

At the oak of Tabor he was to meet three men going up to God at Bethel, one carrying three loaves, another three kids and the third a bottle of wine. They were to salute him and give him two loaves, which he was to receive of their hands.

This also was no new experience, for Bethel was the central sanctuary of his tribe, whither he had probably gone up many a time himself carrying just such offerings, 'and the oak of Tabor with its fresh, vivid green against the brown upland had probably been a landmark to him from childhood. An oak tree, with its verdant, whispering shade, in a landscape where all else is parched and brown, is so impressive a sight that it has often attracted to itself the worship which is due only to the Power who sustains it. This sense of the wonder of nature around came into Saul's heart as he saw it, but the men with their offerings carried his thoughts beyond to the worship of God above. He felt, even if he could not express it, the same lesson as our Lord taught from the lilies of the field, clothed by God's hand in a splendour greater than Solomon in his glory.

Then the two loaves, on their way to the sanctuary and diverted to his use, became a sacrament to attest that he who fights God's battles can trust God for the resources, though only, it may be, in daily bare provision. There are but two loaves, one for himself and one for his servant. Of the kids and the wine nothing is offered. Here was the promise of the strictest necessaries of life for himself and those who should rise at his bidding. But there were no superfluities, no luxuries. Saul, who was to secure to every one in Israel the produce of his flock and make his vine a shelter under which he might sit unafraid, was himself to do his work on bread and drink of the brook by the way, glad to know he would come through, and not greatly caring how. In that spirit he was to take these two loaves, gladly and gratefully, as the sign that a man whose soul is nourished by the sense of high enterprise can be content to be assured of each day's sufficient bread, not only in mere food, but in every other kind of supply.

This is the faith in God which has always equipped captains over His inheritance. They have always seen the superfluities, and though they of all men most deserved them, they have seldom enjoyed them, but, being absorbed in high creative tasks, they do not suffer envy nor turn aside to forage for better rations. All the world's greatest benefactors, the men who have spent themselves to make life beautiful or just or good, have had little of the kids and the wine.

Possibly the chief reason why our successes lately

were so merely material, our work in every higher department so unoriginal, our leaders so lacking the stamp of greatness, was the absence of this sign of the two loaves, set in the wonder of nature around and the adoration of God above.

As a third sign Saul would come to the hill of God, where is the garrison of the Philistines. From the high place—the sanctuary at the top—a company of prophets come down meeting him, with a psaltery and a tabret, and a pipe and a harp before them. They prophesy and he prophesies with them. Then he is finally and completely turned into another man.

The first sign showed the true scope of Saul's enterprise, and the second the true nature of his resources. Yet many a man has had a splendid vision, enriched with all the hues of human interest, of what he might do, and has not asked much for himself in the doing of it, and it has still come to nothing, because he could not at once look steadfastly in the face of stern reality and lift up his heart in prophetic hope. But this third sign united for Saul the seemingly incompatible experiences of a new realisation of the power and oppression of the garrison of the enemy on his native hill and the hope of deliverance by the might and goodness of the God whose sanctuary still hallowed it. And what is the final authentic sign of victory, if not that our native hill, being also God's hill, cannot forever be the seat of violence and wrong? Nor is hope ever sure till it vindicate itself where depressing realities meet us oftenest and harass us most.

This sight was least of all new. Every day, as he went about his work, it had been under his eyes. What is here called Gibeah of God or God's Hill, is elsewhere called Gibeah of Saul or Saul's Hill. On the very spot where he had played as a child and pastured his cattle and tilled his ancestral acres was the garrison of the Philistines, the very fortress from which his native land suffered base oppression. It was as familiar to him as his own homestead; and perhaps it had been as unquestioned hitherto, just as we accept the hovels unfit for human habitation at our back-door or the long bar at the end of our street as the eternal order of things.

But now the scales of custom fell from his eyes and the fresh glory of the spot that was his by birth and habitation shone out upon him. By every experience that had gone to the making of him in God's image it was for him, above every other place on earth, God's Hill, on which the garrison of the Philistines was no matter of course, but a fresh desecration of its sacredness every day the sun rose upon it. There beside it was the high place, God's own immemorial sanctuary, and now he felt with every fibre of his manhood that the two had no right to exist together.

Yet, without the other sight which gladdened his eyes, he might have felt this only with blind and impotent rage. From this most basely contaminated,

yet most sacred seat of his own ancestral home
came down a company, with no lament of vanished
glories or wailing over present oppressions, but
adding to their own cheerful voices every instrument of joyful and soul-stirring music on which
they had been able to lay their hands. Thus they
proclaimed themselves prophets, living in God's
great triumphant future though willing to abide
God's time, aware even now of the wisdom of His
discipline but never doubting the certainty of His
deliverance.

What wonder that Saul responded to their inspiration and won for the moment a prophetic insight into
the great, heroic, divine elements in the heart of his
people to which he could confidently appeal, and became such a man that, though, when it was a question
of honour, he hid himself like a child, when it was
a question of danger, he went to meet it as a lover
goes to his mistress.

Under this inspiration he made such an impression of lovableness and power and self-forgetfulness
on all who followed him, that they never lost for
him, in spite of all his later sorrowful failure, their
affection and regard, but sang over his grave the
lament of David which associated him with Jonathan,
the son who reminded them of his father in the
bright days of his youthful and happy and modest
valour, as 'lovely and pleasant in their lives, yet
swifter than eagles and stronger than lions.'

All great deliverances that ever come to the world

are wrought by such men as Saul when God's signs came upon him. Nor is there any limit to their possible achievement when they go forward, well knowing what they do, in the teeth of all prudent calculation of visible forces, assured only of a might which works for the free soul of man and the gracious things of human lives and for a righteous rule between man and man. They have no need to have pointed out to them the occasion which serves their purpose or to be directed in the right use of it when it comes, or to be encouraged in the faith to venture on its call, for they have in them the signs of love and faith and hope which enable them to discern its opportunity, seize upon its advantage and open their hearts to its inspiration. They are no visionaries, but see the bitter, distressing, discouraging reality, with a clearness eyes blinded by custom never attain. But they are men of vision, and they see that the final power is in the heart of man God has made in His own image and in the God who can touch it to a finer emotion capable of great and splendid consecration.

When life seems to be passing us in drab monotony and dull trivialities, and we feel our days are barren because we have been denied the opportunities lavished upon more fortunate men, is the true reason that the occasion has never come or is it that we are without the signs for discovering and using it? Like Saul, when he had lost these signs and become another man, worse for the loss of what he once possessed, when his joy in service and strength in responsibility had changed to a settled gloomy envy and weak frenzy of suspicion for the honour of his own estate, we meet even great occasions with dismay and handle them as mere soothsayer's destiny and fortune, as an accident merely happening to us and not as an event appointed us for ourselves to turn to good and for manifesting to all men that God is with us.

Has occasion, thus judged, ever greatly served the wisest and best, the true benefactors of our race? Socrates found his occasions as a barefooted private soldier on a winter campaign or talking to young men in the open market-place or at social gatherings which without him would have been frivolous and not very sober entertainments. Paul found his among small groups of humble people at a prayer-meeting, or in lawcourts with an atmosphere more of legality than justice, or in a prison-cell with no accessories save an occasional humble friend and writing material. Shakespeare's special occasion was his father's bankruptcy, and Wordsworth's nothing but plain country-folk and the hills and the sky.

But above all, how did occasion serve the life which wrought man's supreme deliverance, and that not only in its great and heroic moments, but in its every word and work? There was nothing in it which might not happen to any of us, and very little which does not happen to all of us almost every day. A few great ones of the earth Jesus did encounter, but to little profit. The people with whom His occasions of wisdom and power and love came were humble, ordinary, ill-educated, hard-working, and not specially gifted in any way. Which of us would find occasions for penetrating judgment, sublime teaching, supreme action, when we saw weeds flourishing in a field, or children playing in a square, or a wastrel going to the dogs, or a woman who had sold her virtue, or a man of bad repute seized with a fit of curiosity? Yet these are our occasions exactly as they were His. Nor may you suppose you would make more out of the occasions in His life which you have not met than out of those which you have. Relentless and implacable enemies, public opposition and secret intrigues, an unjust trial and a shameful and cruel execution are not what we mean by occasion serving us.

Nor did He ever act except as occasion served. He had no programme except the right use of life as it came, and especially His right service of men as He met them. The only event He ever planned—the triumphal entry—has its significance from the contrast with all the rest of His doings. All His life happened, if you like to put it so, by accident, but He did, what no one else ever did, He took out of every occasion all that was in it, so that all His life, and not merely some particular heroic moment, was God's occasion and the manifestation that the Father was with Him.

This supreme use of occasions available for us

all He made by having, not in one moment of exaltation but uninterruptedly all His days, the signs open to us all. He knew and valued every one He met—and not least what others thought the lost soul, as he valued himself, or rather as his Father in Heaven knew and valued him. With the fine penetration of perfect sympathy He knew what was in man, and, whether He was stern or gentle, peremptory or patient, He never made a mistake in dealing with anyone.

No trapping ever stood between him and the soul of man, and just as little did any material obstacle stand between Him and the spiritual ends He set before Himself. Poverty had no terrors for Him, care for the future no burden, misrepresentation no dismay, and the might of men and the fear of agony or death never turned Him from the way that had in it His true call and opportunity.

All this He did in no dubiety about the evil in the heart of man, the hypocrisy in his religion, the rule of the Father of Lies in his society. Yet there is not a note of querulousness, or shrill impotent rage, but the most essential and unchanging quality of His spirit is a calm strong note of triumph, with a quiet undertone of the blessedness of love's kingdom, as if in His life all the stars of God sang together, and never for a moment as if the highest men knew might only be a great perhaps. The reason was not only that God was with Him, but that He was in the Father and the Father in Him, so that He lived unchangeably and luminously in the light of the knowledge that no event in life could be so evil as not to be God's occasion.

To-day, more anxiously perhaps than ever in the history of our people, we are looking for captains over God's inheritance, and our minds fly to great men and great occasions. But, if we truly looked for them in the name of the Captain of our Salvation, should we not look instead for God's signs to teach us all to see and use all occasions in the might of His succour? These signs are still the old authentic signs which yet make all things new, even love and faith and hope. Were we by them made other men, our occasions would serve us as well as anything more exalted we might imagine, even for the great and high deliverances we think we need. If it be so that God anoint us to be kings for such high tasks, we shall not need to shrink or be dismayed. But for working out the true salvation of our land from the powers of evil, and for emancipating all that is free and high and holy in the souls of men, He has anointed us all to be kings and priests unto Him: and He requires a heroic task from us, even if it be only in our own homes, where perhaps all our best occasions are found.

We shall never see them or find God's help in them without His signs, enabling us to look through the outward appearance to the heart of things and especially to the hearts of men. But then all occasions will be at our command.

XIV

WRONG WAITING FOR GOD

MARK xi. 13. 'For the time of figs was not yet.'

THIS whole incident seems strangely unlike the convincing reasonableness of the rest of the Gospels. How could One, for whom the shooting blade was a symbol of the Kingdom of God and the lily was arrayed beyond Solomon in all his glory, blast the promise of anything that grows? But these words read like the very essence of unreason; for why should a tree be cursed for not bearing fruit out of season? How could He who was so patient with failure, even after it had enjoyed every opportunity, pass a judgment so hasty and so unjust?

The lesson, moreover, seems to strike a false note in a ministry, which, though carried through in a few crowded months, is singularly free from driving and hurry, and possessed of leisure to observe the flowers and the children and the fields and the sky. Above all how does it accord with the patience and quiet insight which enabled Jesus to deal adequately with the needs of all who sought His help? Nothing else suggests that, even under the strain of those closing days, He fell from this gentle reasonableness and began to require men to produce fruit out of the course of nature, to force the doors

of opportunity, to live lives richer than their experience, to render service beyond the growth of their
souls. Such a violent spirit of haste has often possessed
His Church, but it never assailed the gracious spirit
of its Founder.

Nor, rightly understood, are these words an exception. Just what seems unreasonable in them is
what gives reasonableness to the whole incident.

The warning it conveys becomes clear when we
realise that the time of the fruit harvest represents
the time of the fruition of God's purpose in the
earth, the coming of His Kingdom. It was addressed
to the thought in the mind of the disciples that the
Day of the Lord was at hand and that they had only
to await its coming in unproductive impatience.

This coming of the Kingdom our Lord describes
in many figures. It is a feast at which He will sit
with His disciples, love's fulfilment when the rule of
violence shall be ended, treasure found after weary
search, a jewel purchased at the price of all we
possess. But the favourite figure is this of the harvest,
which is to justify all God's husbandry, with its use
of the pruning-knife and its disregard to shelter
which cannot keep out the storm without keeping
out also the sun and the rain.

Our Lord taught that this Kingdom was at hand,
and He meant the expectation to be supreme in
the lives of His followers. They were to lift up
their eyes and see the fields white to the harvest;
and, knowing that it was both near and sure, they

were to pray the Lord of the harvest to send forth other labourers, and not themselves to sit still with folded hands.

Our supreme temptations lie very near our supreme inspirations: and this is no exception to the rule. The wrong way of waiting upon the God who will, in their season, provide the fruits of the earth, the way which ungirds the loins and unnerves the hands, is not far apart from the right way, the way which inspires and braces and stirs the heart.

At this moment the disciples were waiting in the wrong way. Their hope of the Kingdom had ceased to be an inspiration and had become an enervation. They asked only when it would come, not how they should rightly await its coming. Now as later, the first question always hovering on their lips was, 'Wilt thou at this time restore the kingdom to Israel?' The disciples were spiritual men, and that was no merely material hope, but, if they sought a spiritual kingdom, it was in unspiritual ways. It was a kingdom that was within, but they expected it wholly from without; it was a victory of righteousness, but they expected only a victory of power; it was a call to service and a temper of humility, but they thought that they had only to wait till they were called to rule. They might still be said to live by hope, but it was a hope which was merely marking time, a hope which counted for nothing in the interval. That it would be a time of special call and opportunity they did not dream. God was to bring in His Kingdom in all power and splendour, and their patience was to be exercised only in waiting with upward look and folded hands.

Their Lord, on the contrary, meant this hope to be a trumpet-call to high enterprise. The Lord God omnipotent reigns, therefore they also must reign as kings; His triumph was secure, therefore they now must be more than conquerors. Their thinking was not useless nor their working vain, for the very reason that the result of God's thinking and working would in time appear. The assurance that He works the willing and the doing was to inspire them to work out their own salvation, not only with fear and trembling, but with confidence and peace.

The incident is a warning, therefore, not to undervalue the times of more limited blessing and the less obvious working of God, and, especially, not to neglect the present with such opportunity as is offered and such success as is accorded. Though the Kingdom of God may have come only in some small measure for our own souls, we must bring forth now, in such measure as our special privileges admit, and not wait to attain in the general procession of the seasons. As the specially sheltered tree heralds the autumn by bearing as though summer had completed its work in all the land, so we must herald its coming for the world by showing that it is already within ourselves.

If that be the meaning of the offending phrase 'The time of figs was not yet,' we may now see why this incident appears at this solemn point in the sublimest of all tragedies.

At first sight the fate of a fig-tree seems utterly beneath the dignity of the occasion, when such vast human issues were being decided. We cannot suppose it is introduced, like the lighter scenes in the tragedies of Shakespeare, to relieve the mind for a moment, in order, by a quickened feeling and a sense of contrast, to make it more sensitive to the agony that follows. For that purpose it is far too sombre. But it does come in for another reason, which Shakespeare also well understood, that when the feelings are deeply moved by great events, the most trivial incident may have the deepest significance.

Jesus was going up to Jerusalem to His last great day of appeal and conflict. He was fasting, and even a handful of figs would have sustained His strength for a task which was to try His physical powers to the utmost. The leaves promised fruit, but He found none: and no wealth of fruit any tree in the world could ever produce would have the value of the poorest handful of figs which would have served the Master's need in that supreme hour.

Most of you have something in your own experience to help you to understand how that moment of disappointment would live on in the memory of the disciples. You recall perhaps some last wish, some last look of disappointment, appealing to you

out of the gathering shadows of the great darkness,
which you could not meet, and which, even after your
deepest sorrow has changed to tender and gracious
recollection, still comes with sharp pain every time
it returns to your memory.

The fig-tree itself need not detain us. In Palestine,
it is said, a ripe fig or two might be found at any
season. Or this particular tree may have enjoyed
such special advantages of sun and shade, that,
had its energies not all been spent on leaf, it might
have had ripe fruit. And, in any case, it had no
fruit at all, which is a singular thing in a fig-tree
at any time. All we need concern ourselves about
is that our Lord had reason to expect fruit, that the
appearance of the tree encouraged His hope, and
that He found only the luxuriance of foliage which
is the fore-runner of death.

The lesson, which is our true concern, is the
very simple one which the stirring of new life every
spring-time teaches. Then, and not in the autumn,
the issue is decided. You go out in the March
weather and you see a timid blossom in a sheltered
nook. You may say, Here is a rash venture likely
to be nipped in the bud by the late frost or to
shiver to death in the east wind. But you may also
say, Here is the potency of summer already on its
way. The spring is a call, which, if it is not answered
at once, will never be answered at all. Where life
is stirring, it is not only striving to produce fruit,
but to produce it at the earliest moment. If it will

not hasten to brave the sharp spring winds with blossom, it will gladden no harvest, either soon or late, with fruit. And it must respond to its own warmth and shelter, and not wait till all the earth is filled with sunshine.

The poet speaks of shining like a good deed in a naughty world. But the venture of faith is more even than that. It is the wave which rises higher on the shore, because it has behind it the whole might of the tidal billow; or, as here, it is the first ripe fruit which comes with the potency of the ripening year. And when we think of it, what figure speaks of vaster, more transforming power than this quiet influence of the seasons, this invigorating ally of all that lives!

It means that we must embrace our own opportunities and not wait for opportunity in general; use our special warmth and shelter and not wait till the sun warms all winds and bathes all nature in heat; ourselves herald the autumn and not wait to be its tardy result.

It is the great, urgent, everyday, insistent lesson of life, that to sit waiting for fuller opportunity is to miss all opportunity, late as well as soon. You may not be daunted by less favourable conditions and fold your hands and merely wait for better, but you must do the little you can when circumstances are adverse ere you can expect to use them to better purpose when they are favourable, just as you must consecrate your powers when they are feeble if you are to employ them effectively in their maturity.

Yet it is more than this, because it is not a demand, but an inspiration. When there stirs in your heart the vaguest desire to help your struggling brethren, when you put forth the worst directed effort to help them, when some gentle and kind impulse hides itself modestly amid the visible pretence and show of your lives, you have not discovered merely an untimely blossom, which will bear little fruit with the best success and most likely suffer blight in the chill social winds around you, but you have the promise that God's summer draws nigh, a foretaste of all the warmth and fruitfulness of the Kingdom of God, of which you may be sure that God needs the fruit if it prosper, and that He will see the promise of life in it, even though it fail.

We can now see why our Lord goes on to speak about the faith which removes mountains. It is not merely because the fig-tree has died at His word. Any of us could kill a fig-tree: none of us can remove a mountain. And the spirit of that appeal would be equally unlike our Lord. He would have been giving a sign in the very form He always repudiated. But He too is thinking of the coming of the Kingdom of God: and He warns the disciples that while their way of looking for it is death, His way is life and victory. Nothing, He means, need dismay you, nothing be deemed impossible, because you are producing fruit with the ripening year on your side, because the Kingdom of God is at hand and all you do is already of its power. Only use this hope of a fuller day which is coming as an inspiration and not as an excuse, and nothing is beyond your reach.

The handful of early fruit which might have stayed the Master's hunger on the day of His supreme conflict, and which was not forthcoming, is typical of most of our human failures. The highway is never made, because none were found to beat the track.

In all life it is the pioneer who counts. A great many people could make as good poetry as Cowper, but in which of them could be heard a new note of nature and truth, heralding a new age of song? Any of us can go to America to-day, but that takes nothing from the merit of Columbus. The pope may be set right to-day as a pastime, but that is because Wicliffe did it when it seemed a madness. With a little assurance, we could any of us preach at Athens to-day, but that detracts nothing from the splendour of the amazing solitary figure of Paul facing the Areopagus.

The act which has everything on its side—knowledge and custom and human approval—does no mighty work in the earth. Yet knowing that, we may still, by some illusion, think we have no call to go ahead of the crowd. Every young man worth his salt dreams of being a pioneer in something. But he excuses himself from beginning, by the reflection that the time is not yet. Most of us take up the attitude that nothing can be done till the current sets strongly in our favour and bears us along, almost in our own despite. As children we think things will happen by the mere force of growing up; as young people that we must grow wise and worthy by the mere process of the years; as persons of middle life, that age, by the mere process of decay, will make us unworldly and good, because it will leave us no temptation to be otherwise. We forget that the future has no promise which does not declare itself in present achievement, and that nothing ever comes by mere lapse of time except dissolution. We forget that we can grow in folly as in wisdom, in worldliness and pride as well as in humility and love. We forget, in short, that the significant time for everything is not the time when all impulses are in our favour, and all votes on our side, but is, on the contrary, the time when we see only half truths, follow doubtful glimpses of reality, meet cold indifference and hard rebuffs, that, in short, the significant time, the time which determines all harvests, is the opening year with the bite of winter still in it, and not autumn with its breathless calms and its mellow heat.

This incident, then, is a demand for the pioneer, and in it, throughout, his supreme value is assumed. Yet the lesson does not preach to us merely that we should all endeavour to be pioneers. It speaks of faith and not of effort, of the Rule of God and not of the will of man, of a power which can make even us ordinary people, without high courage, clear initiative, or great originality, true pioneers of God's Kingdom. The venture of faith is not to thrust ourselves in the face of events, and carve our way through a hostile world, but to discern God's large purposes and feel the inspiration of His new world. And it is because Jesus Christ means for us this new vision and inspiration, and not a mere exhortation to brace ourselves and steel our hearts, that we speak of faith in Him and not merely of belief in what He teaches.

A few weeks after this event the Disciples themselves showed how they had learned the lesson. A day came when they stood alone in Jerusalem, face to face with the men who had crucified their Master and with their cause discredited in the eyes of the people. Every counsel of prudence urged delay. God's power had already been manifested to them in the Resurrection, and they had every reason to hope that it would display itself to the world yet more plainly in a new age. Was it not common-sense to wait till this arrived? Yet something had happened in the soul of a fisherman who had known how to be rash but not how to be brave, whose uncultured country accent betrayed his origin and who had no equipment save the faith which enabled him to say the word which removed the mountain, and to say it at the moment. He touched

the hearts of the very men who had been deaf to
the Master's own appeal and he made the very
lips which had cried, 'Crucify Him,' cry out in an
agony of penitence. Had he, on that day, judged
that no prudent and successful effort could be made
till God had done something more to bring in His
Kingdom, had he not forgotten all timidities in the
assurance that the Kingdom of God had come for
his own soul, in righteousness and peace and joy in
the Holy Ghost, then, so far as we can see, it would
have meant death to Peter's faith and, so far as Peter
was concerned, to his Master's cause. As it was,
when Peter had spoken, a new age had come. But
the reason of his heroism was neither courage nor
resolution. It was faith. Peter saw God's new world
and, thinking of nothing else, he simply suffered it
to speak through him: and it spoke effectively, and
spoke in time.

This is what faith in Christ, whose triumph over
death showed Him to be 'a man approved of God,'
meant for Peter. It meant for him that he had
'a Prince and a Saviour' who, he knew, would
found a kingdom in the lives of men. And he knew
because it had already been founded in his own
heart. With that foretaste of its might Peter awaited
its coming, as a pioneer in its van and not as a mere
camp-follower in its rear. What it did for him, it
can do for us, and also in the same way of the inspiration of faith and not the constraining of effort.
It will not ask us to be different persons and to

force the doors of opportunity, but will give us such a sense of the power which is on our side as will enable us to be our true selves, setting before us, always on the latch, a great door and effectual into our true and immediate service.

Our lives mean so little because, while we dream of some peculiar and unique service, the last thing we dream of is of being ourselves unique. We wait for some one else to move, or for some common, concerted action. In religion, above all, we wait for a revival, by which we mean a movement which will carry us off our feet by a great common emotion, and make belief come without thought, and obedience by mere submission to impulse.

How many, at this moment, in every branch of the Church of Christ, are simply saying to themselves, 'The time of figs is not yet.' A few only spend their energies manipulating prophecy to discover the exact date of the Second Coming, which apparently is nearer the less we see of promise in the present time, but many more persons do what is equally futile. They think this is a very worldly age, a very perplexed age, an age in which it is a good deal to keep up any appearance of religious interest at all. Formerly they urged the need of campaigns, and their minds flew to committees and subscriptions and printed programmes. To-day they are full of schemes to be put into operation when our outward troubles are over. All this is a way of saying to God, 'Lord, dost thou at this time restore the kingdom to Israel?' They are willing to organise so that some day it may happen with éclat and commotion, but meantime they do not bethink themselves that the Kingdom of God may have already come for their own souls, and that it can now bring forth its fruit in their own lives, and that the Master is in need of it, as He will never be in later, it may be more inspired, times.

But, even when we do not think in this way, too often our service is merely of effort and not of faith. Our first thought is that we must be quite different persons from what we are, and should have all our dim trusts and gropings replaced by absolute convictions, with all our resolutions passed through a process which will turn them from soft iron into hard steel, and that we should make spacious plans and force ourselves upon far-reaching enterprises and undertake lofty tasks. And what is the result? Usually disappointment, often despair, always mere words and unrealities.

But our real need is just to be what God means us to be, and to go the way God has set before us, and to respond to the appeals God addresses to our own hearts—in short, to allow God's Kingdom to come for our own souls here and now.

The early fruit is produced in the same way as the late, by the plant turning to the light and the heat of the sun. Only it must be sensitive and turn even though the clouds may intervene. We are to respond better to the truth we see and the grace

we feel—and that is all. Our true concern is not
our clearness and certainty, but our sincerity and
simplicity, not our perfect practical guidance, but
our readiness to put our hand to the task that lies
nearest to us, while we await further direction as
God sees good. Not in a view of the whole journey
from the beginning to the end, but in taking each
step as we see it, in the certainty that God directs it
to His own goal, do we serve God.

You need no conspicuous life, no sphere of
notable deeds, nothing beyond the ordinary people
around you and your daily common tasks, if that
be all God require. Yet you must be prepared for
high and hazardous demands, if He make them.
Nor may you expect always a direct and clear call
or trumpet-summons even to the highest, but must
often be content to follow the untrodden perilous
way, aspiring dimly after truth and groping forward
in the way of duty. But does Christ mean for you
that in this poor shrivelled fruit of your lives the
power and glory of God's Kingdom are being
manifested and that it is the summer of His purpose
which is breathing life into your soul? Then you
will be able to be yourself, seeing your own truth
and hearing your own call even in these dim lights
and uncertain voices; and you will no longer wait
to march in companies, or till you are no more
chilled by want of sympathy, repressed by criticism,
or crushed by the sense of the vast, dead forces against
you. Because you know that this dim light and this

humble, hesitating obedience mean that Christ, with all the might and glory of His Kingdom, is on His way, because your life, in short, is a life of faith and not merely of courage and determination, you will show that the Spirit of God is abroad in the earth, and you will be ready with your fruit in the day of the Master's need.

Otherwise, it will be the old story—'Let no man eat fruit of thee from henceforth.' 'The harvest is past and the summer is ended, and we are not saved.'

XV

YOUTH AND AGE

JOHN xxi. 18. 'Verily, verily, I say unto thee, when thou wast young, thou girdedst thyself, and walkedst whither thou wouldest: but when thou shalt be old, thou shalt stretch forth thy hands, and another shall gird thee, and carry thee whither thou wouldest not.'

HERE we have a picture of Peter young and of Peter old, like one of those days, so familiar to our climate, which is radiant with sunshine from dawn to noon, then steeped in fogs till night descend. But is that other than the picture of all youth and age? Perhaps in this very typical nature of his life and experience we find the secret of Peter's perennial interest. He is just our more virile selves, in whom we see intensely and decisively what we ourselves are only feebly and vaguely. When he was young, he was really young, being buoyant, enterprising, free; and, when he was old, he was really old, being limited, constrained, distressed.

'When thou wast young, thou girdedst thyself.' In our modern figure he was ever ready to take his coat off for any task in hand, and needed none to help him off with it. Most mistakes he could make, but not the supreme mistake of allowing life's opportunities to slip past not used at all.

It may not be youth's privilege to be always

wise, but it ought to be youth's equipment to be always enterprising. To lack this is, at any age, to be already decrepit; and to set out in life with the idea of dodging the primal curse, that anything worth doing is to be done only in the sweat of one's brow, is merely to be born old.

Nor is it enough to be ready to face tasks when they are imposed on us. To be really young we must turn the curse into a joy, girding ourselves and going out to seek adventure, and not hanging up decision till others have made up their minds and decided for us.

By this measure Peter was pre-eminently young. Before others had grasped the situation, he had already started to act on it. A fine independence, with rapid decision and promptness of word and action, proved him in those days daringly, originally, energetically young.

In days of multitudinous societies and fellowships and movements, and generally of acting in crowds, even the young are in danger of losing this mark of youth. Fellowship is a very fine thing, and youth is essentially clubbable. But the true difference between a crowd and a fellowship, is that, in the former, we help to sweep each other off our feet, and that, in the latter, it is our supreme task to help one another to find our own feet. We can misuse the best helps, and we misuse the best of all human helps—the sympathy of our brethren—when we rely wholly on the enthusiasm around us to gird us for enterprise and high resolve. The result too often is that to sit close together and keep ourselves warm is regarded as the end of religion; whereas youth's true way of being warm is to breast the hill and battle with the storm in its own energy and purpose.

Finally, Peter took off his own coat to his own enterprise. 'Thou girdedst thyself and walkedst whither thou wouldest.'

Things no one else thought of doing Peter did. Into the first confession of Jesus as the Christ he walked, the first offer to die with Him, the first facing of a hostile world that had crucified his Master. Often they were mistaken ways. But what mistakes! 'This be far from thee, Lord.' 'Let us build here three tabernacles.' 'Though I should die with thee, yet will I not deny thee.' Let us remember, even about his denial, that all the others made the same profession, and he alone went far enough to be tempted and to fall.

There above all else is the mark of youth, to stake everything with a high heart upon our own enterprise.

> He either fears his fate too much
> Or his deserts are small,
> That dares not put it to the touch,
> To win or lose it all.

To this reproach Peter was never exposed.

To be young is to feel that the world is before us, with all the multitudinous paths which run to every point of the horizon to choose from, and the one we choose truly ours, courageously to be entered and steadfastly to be followed.

But how few are ever young after that fashion! Most make some timid efforts and then find themselves in the beaten path. At most they seek a newly beaten path, a recent fashion of thought. But, however it afford a pleasant sense of independence and originality, a new heterodoxy is no more one's own path than an ancient orthodoxy. So long as we merely follow and do not choose of our own insight and go on of our own resolution, whether it turn out to be the ancient beaten road or the recent track, we can arrive at no worthy goal. The people God has called to high service have ever had a stout heart for their own untrodden, solitary way.

Have you young people sufficiently before you this sense that you may never measure your opinions or duties by others, and that there is no way in life wholly right for you except your own? There is even some danger at present of regarding a general emotion which seems to set in one direction as the peculiar manifestation of the Holy Spirit. But God's Spirit calls each one to his own life and service; and, if we are all moved to do the same thing in the same way, let us be very chary about ascribing it to the voice of God who has created us all differently after His own image.

Let us make no mistake. It is a fine thing to have been really young. A youth over cautious, fearful of risks, happy only while following the crowd, is not the stuff upon which a Church, or for that matter any noble enterprise, is ever built. The foundation of Christ's Church, as of all else worth building, was not the person who had followed the fashion of the hour or the custom of the age, but the man for whom life was ever a new adventure, who made up his mind and tightened his belt to face the worst in the way he had chosen, and who ever did it with a flash of fresh decision. Here Jesus sees the presence of bed-rock, though the fresh, green sward may have to be torn up and deeply trenched to reveal it. How unlike the superficial judgment which sees it in the man of fixed habit and stolid caution, which is only as though we were deceived by the likeness of shale to stone into seeking under it the enduring granite.

We older people naturally exaggerate the value of experience, as if we grew wise merely by increasing years. But we never grow old to any profit unless we have been first really young.

There is an Italian proverb which says, "Not to know at twenty is never to know, not to do at thirty is never to do, and not to have at forty is never to have." Learning, of course, does not stop at twenty or doing at thirty or acquiring at forty, but, if we miss the insight of twenty or the energy of thirty or have nothing accomplished behind us at forty, the promise even of the longest life is small. Without these fruitful beginnings, the process of growing old is a mere tale of darkening insight, of languishing enterprise, and of increasing poverty of spirit. Get this well into your mind, that till you have first been young with the high hopes, rapid decisions, and tense vigour of youth, you cannot grow old to profit. Better any mistake than the supreme mistake of wasting your life because you were without the brave, indifferent, joyous heart that dared to live.

'But when thou shalt be old, thou shalt stretch forth thy hands, and another shall gird thee, and carry thee whither thou wouldest not.' All the spontaneity, all the ardour, all the enterprise gone! The inevitable alone left, and such poor submission to it as we cannot avoid! Not getting what we like, but doing our poor best to like what we get! This truly is being and feeling old.

> Surely the golden hours are turning grey
> And dance no more, and vainly strive to run:
> I see their white locks streaming in the wind—
> Each face is haggard as it looks at me,
> Slow turning in the constant clasping round,
> Storm-driven.

The very thought of it chills your blood. Is life, which was so buoyant with the call to follow your own bent and high resolve, to be reduced to this mill-track round which nearly all your seniors seem to tread? All kinds of hands gird them. Even little infants have giant hands for the purpose. You know that a vast number go on day by day accepting all kinds of dull drudgeries, driven by needs not their own. You feel chilly and grown old already at the thought of it. How shall you also be girded by others and carried whither you would not, when you have been properly fitted into your groove! Is it strange that a fierce rebellion against this inevitable subjection occasionally glows through your veins?

Yet the question of how you will submit is even greater than the question of how you will choose. Inevitable in some way submission will be, but whether it be the mere surrender of weakness or the consecration of peace depends on how you grow old. All alike we must grow old if we live, but we are very far from being alike in our way of growing old. One way is to shrivel up and become too small for life. But there is also the other way of finding life become too large for us.

That is the difference which decides for you the value of old age. Does constraint come upon you, because you become small or because life becomes great?

Now let us look at Peter as he grows old. We see him faced by a new age which he never was able to understand, and in which he never could choose his own way and walk in it. Only on the compulsion of a vision, could he bring himself to enter the house of a Gentile; only when he saw that Cornelius had received the same gift as himself, could he cease withstanding God; only when openly rebuked by Paul, did he see the inconsistency of calling the Gentiles brethren in word and denying it in deed. Never did he rise to

Paul's vision or follow even what he saw with Paul's freedom.

Part of the failure was due just to old age. Had he been a younger man, he too might have seen the vision of a universal Christianity, and have set aside boldly all that stood in its way. Yet we must remember that to Peter was given the mission to the Jews even as to Paul the mission to the Gentiles; and his perplexities arose from this task, seeing how every step he took to a more comprehensive fellowship meant the alienation of those he sought to win. Further, we must remember that Peter remained for Paul one God wrought for as truly as for himself, an apostle to the Jew, yet, like himself, to be appropriated by the Gentile, the first witness to the Resurrection, as he himself was the last. Nor perhaps was his task less necessary than Paul's, for how would the Gospel have fared had he not preserved the loyalty of those who, like himself, could only see a step at a time, and even take it only by the manifest compulsion of God? That compulsion, moreover, he never opposed. However much the issue was forced upon him, in the end he stretched forth his hands, and allowed himself to be carried even whither he would not.

But this supreme surrender was not attained merely by the limitations of age. It was due to three experiences which had so expanded the meaning of life that he knew he could not find his way at all except by the compulsion of God's will.

First, he had learned his own weakness. He had thought that no power on earth could make him deny his Master, and he had succumbed to the scoff of a servant-maid. None of us know ourselves till we have made this discovery; and, once it is made, no one walks the ways of life again with the same easy confidence.

Second, he had learned the meaning of the Cross. The last word the Master Himself could say was, 'Not my will but thine be done': and Peter had seen this submission turned into God's own victory. Who that has ever shared this triumph can be sure again that his own way is best?

Finally, he had seen a larger vision of the Kingdom of God. Dim it may have been and its horizons beyond his sight, but how great and spiritual it was compared with the restoration of the kingdom to Israel for which he once hoped! So measureless indeed had it become that God alone could show him the way to serve it.

We too have entered on a new age. Those of you who are young may obtain a clear vision of its purpose, and see your own way in the midst of it and gird your own loins and walk in it by a way you see stretching clear before you. And if so, you must serve like Paul, not turning from high demands, nor hesitating to form large plans, nor in any way being disobedient to the heavenly vision. But for many of us it will be too late for this way of fresh under-standing and new resolve, and all the more if life has brought us already large responsibilities and urgent service. Like Peter, we shall often doubt the result and feel constantly the sense of loss. But it is God, and not man, who sees the end from the beginning. Wherefore, the last question about us is not how do we determine, but how do we submit. When we live in sincerity and are compelled to recognise that the belief we fear is true or the course of action we think hazardous is right, the Master Himself girds us. Do we stretch forth our hands, and allow ourselves to be carried even though it continue to be whither we would not? As the last resort the wisest of us will come to this. The vision fades, and we must accept the compulsion of conviction and duty and submit hour by hour to the demands of God's will. At the end of the day there is no other way in which God can to the last be glorified.

In a special sense this saying is applied to Peter's actual death. But only a death of surrender which crowns a life of surrender can glorify God. Death must be the seal of our lives, even as Christ's fulfilling of all righteousness on the Cross was the seal and perfection of His life, ere it counts in God's service, right dying perfecting right living.

Regarding Peter's death there is a tradition, which, if not actual history, is at least good commentary on our text. Peter, we are told, was present in Rome when the first great persecution arose. He was persuaded to flee, it is said, for the apostolic reason of further service. But Peter was a very human person in respect of his own fears, and still more in respect of the sorrows of others. And even age could not wholly alter his old impulsive ways. But as he went out of the gate he met the Master going in. "Whither goest Thou?" Peter asked. "I go again to be crucified," was the reply. Peter accepted the rebuke and returned to obey the charge, "Feed my flock," at the cost of the cross; even as his Master. Then the old question "Lovest thou Me?" was answered, as it had never been even in all his free and active and buoyant youth. While the hand ready to open had shut, that ready to close had opened: and the greatest of all acts of service to the glory of God was the last. True he was girded by others, and he had no choice but to submit to what was for him also a cup of agony, but he stretched forth his hands, and, in that act, his whole soul was given in final and complete surrender, in utter trust and love.

For you too the inevitable day will come. It will gird you with violence and carry you whither your soul shudders to go. You are not called to choose death or love it or even to be free from the shadow of its loneliness and uncertainty and terror. Yet at that moment your whole life's submission may be crowned. If you then surrender all earthly things at last willingly into the hands of God, you will glorify God in death as never in life. What all your life could only imperfectly strive after, will thus be utterly completed. May that not be the supreme meaning of death? And, if so, will it not, because it is the perfect glorifying of God, be the suitable way into His Eternal Glory?

Straightway I was 'ware
So weeping, how a mystic shape did move
Behind me, and drew me backward by the hair;
And a voice said in mastery while I strove,—
'Guess now who holds thee!' 'Death,' I said. But there
The silver answer rang,—'Not death but Love.'

XVI

A NAME OF APPEARANCE
AND A NAME OF REALITY

JEREMIAH xx. 3. 'The Lord hath not called thy name Pashur, but Magor-missabib.'

In a review of an American autobiography I found, as near as I can recall it, the following quotation: 'Except a passage or two of Emerson, nothing ever stirred me so much in my youth as the following extract, in Mrs Austen's *Fragments from German Prose Authors*, from Heinzemann, an author of whom I never read another word: "Be and continue poor, young man, while others around you grow rich by fraud and disloyalty; be without place and power, while others beg their way upwards; bear the pain of disappointed hopes, while others gain the accomplishment of theirs by flattery; forgo the gracious pressure of the hand for which others cringe and crawl; wrap yourself in your virtue and seek a friend and your daily bread. If you have in such a course grown grey with unblenched honour, bless God and die." Yet one should temper this with the fine saying of Thoreau, that he did not wish to practise self-denial any more than was quite necessary.'

I have made this long quotation because it sets

forth for us the difference between the characters
and successes of these two men, Pashur and
Jeremiah. Both started together, both were sons of
priests, both had equal opportunities: and Jeremiah
was not the one with less ability or feebler character.
Yet Pashur found popularity and ease the way to
overflowing success, while Jeremiah found poverty
and pain and the hatred which is much worse to
bear, the only way to true manhood. The issue of
it is that Jeremiah sits in the stocks, the object of
scorn and ridicule to every passer-by, and Pashur
is in a position to order it to be done.

Here is something which actually takes place in
life: and the meaning of it is worth inquiring into
and the lesson of it worth pondering. Neither
Jeremiah nor Pashur wished to practise self-denial
any more than was quite necessary. Nor should
anyone ever practise self-denial any more than is
quite necessary. The sole difference between them
lay in the kind of necessity each acknowledged.
And that is the sole difference between any of us.
What for us is quite necessary? Is it only what is
physically necessary—the compulsion of the body,
or is it what is spiritually necessary—the compulsion of the conscience? What man calls us is
chiefly determined by the former; what God calls
us—the infinitely more important consideration—is
determined wholly by the latter.

In those old days people did not choose names
for their children by the sound but by the sense.

The meaning, they thought, ought to be significant of the person who bore the name. Even a name of infancy thus represented parental bias and training. And as names were not committed to the iron custody of the registrar, they could be changed to suit later developments of character and fortune.

To this significance of names Jeremiah refers in our text. The origin of Pashur has been sought in our day as far away as Egypt, but Jeremiah found it nearer home. Pashur the son of Immer he derived from ordinary Hebrew words which make them mean, 'Prosperity all Round' the son of 'The Talker.'

Think of that in plain English. Think of it as one of those old Puritan names like Son of Humility Ford. Put an ordinary English surname to it. Prosperity all Round Ford! What an auspicious name with which to set out in the world! What a popular name it would become, were English parents to take to saying what they think!

Then he was the son of Immer, The Talker. No virtue in him would ever lose effect from lack of a trumpeter, nor any promotion go past him for want of someone to keep asking for it. If your chief business in life is to get on, Immer, The Talker, is quite clearly the person to have for a father. You must not think that it is only in our enlightened days that there were rising young men in the Church or that they had to wait for the era of the religious periodical to have their praises sounded.

And Immer had good reason to be satisfied and to feel that none of his talk had missed its mark. The career of his son was indeed prosperity all round, till he became chief officer of the House of the Lord, thus attaining the very top of his profession. And it is marvellous how ambitions, high and low, do succeed, if only a man follow them persistently and be well supported by his friends.

But if this was the career of Pashur, what might not have been predicted for Jeremiah? In comparison Pashur was a quite commonplace person, with the kind of specially uninteresting commonplaceness which concentration upon the business of getting on begets in men. While Pashur was only a master of smooth and comfortable platitude, Jeremiah had the great gift of the preacher, the power of the winged, the unforgettable word. Had he not imagination, insight, pathos? And are not they the qualities which sway men, and make for success in any calling?

Alas for him, however, his name is not Prosperity all Round, the son of The Talker, but Jeremiah, 'The Lord shall Appoint,' the son of Hilkiah, 'The Lord is my Portion.' Therein lies the difference in character and career.

Manifestly Jeremiah's first mistake in the way of getting on in the world was his father. To regard the Lord seriously as one's portion is apt to make a man forgo other more tangible portions both for himself and his children. And equally clearly his second mistake was with himself. His name was 'The Lord shall Appoint,' and the man who takes that seriously is very apt to find the Lord not appointing prosperity all round, but quite other things.

There you have the secret of their lives. It lies in the necessities which determine them. Pashur will appoint for himself, and nothing will stand in his way except sheer outward obstacle. Jeremiah will have the Lord appoint, and everything will stand in his way that is not utterly veracious and just. Pashur will only be defeated if circumstances are too strong for him. No other necessity in the world could demand from him self-denial. But upon Jeremiah another necessity is laid of an entirely different order, one which makes circumstances a quite secondary and even unimportant consideration.

The difference appears at once in their preaching. Pashur is a shallow enough person, but one fact about mankind he has thoroughly grasped—the very far reaching one that sugar is sweet in the mouth. He built on that as the bottom fact in the universe. He preached smooth things, telling his hearers that they were the most admirable kind of people, whose privileges showed how warmly God approved of them, and how, as He was the God of Israel, He could not afford to do anything but protect them and cherish them and add to their blessings. You can imagine what a sweet and gracious preacher his audiences found him and how good and religious it would make them feel, and what flutterings of approval would pass among them, and what a wanton harrowing of their feelings and desecration of their sanctuary it would seem when Jeremiah, the blunt, rude man, called all this lies.

But when Jeremiah preached, he had no ear at all for the voice of his hearers asking for what they wanted. The sole voice he heard was the voice of the Lord appointing the truth. Then he had only awful, heart shaking, soul shattering things to say. 'Thus saith the Lord of Hosts: Even so will I break this people and this city, as one breaketh a potter's vessel that cannot be made whole again: and they shall bury in Topheth till there be no place to bury.' Never in any age could that be popular preaching. We ought to be amazed at the moderation of Jeremiah's contemporaries that they merely put him in the stocks and dropped him into a pit. Our national temper on quite modern occasions makes it safe to say that we should have been less restrained, particularly if we suspected that what he said was true. Not by any means do the fates of Jeremiah and Pashur belong exclusively to a vanished antiquity.

Pashur, we read, as soon as he learned what Jeremiah preached about, scourged him and set him in the stocks in the most public place he could find, there to reflect on the folly of his ways and consider how his message might be made fitter for polite ears. And with Pashur's view of what was quite necessary before a man needed to practise self-denial, what method of persuasion could have been more effective? Unfortunately for the result, Jeremiah's view of what was quite necessary was of a wholly different order.

There in the stocks in the high gate of Benjamin in the Temple Jeremiah sat all day a target for the gibes and the missiles of the thoughtless, scoffing, malicious crowd that thronged past. And there, when they had all gone, he sat solitary with his own thoughts all through the night, with the purple parallels of the lash stiffening on his back in the chilly night air.

It was an occasion for thinking seriously of one's life; and Jeremiah thought of his as seriously as even Pashur could have desired. He also did not wish to practise self-denial any more than was quite necessary. He too could have won and could have enjoyed prosperity. Above all he too could have loved his friends. Yet this man, with genius, with ardent purpose, with unswerving steadfastness, with all the qualities which can set men on the summit of life's ambition, arrived now at the time of life when his gifts might have brought him wealth, honour, troops of friends, is here poor and scorned and hated and whipped and pilloried, like a mendicant or a criminal.

Jeremiah saw it all, saw it as clearly as Pashur's heart could desire, saw it till he burst forth in that strange, passionate cry: 'O Lord thou hast deceived

me and I was deceived: thou art stronger than I
and hast prevailed: I am become a laughing-stock
all the day, everyone mocketh me...the word of the
Lord is made a reproach unto me and a derision all
the day...I heard the defaming of many, terror on
every side. All my familiar friends watched for my
halting.'

To lie like Pashur could not so much as enter
into his thought. To be guilty of complicity in his
country's fate, saying, 'Ye are all good and worthy
people for whom God can have nothing but blessing
in store,' was not conceivable for him under any
pressure of violence. Might he not, however, hold
his peace? That might not give him the highest
seat in the Temple with its popularity and honour,
but it might at least save him from the lowest with
its scourges and derision. His night of reflection
there makes him think of not making mention of
God or speaking any more in His name, which
was precisely the effect Pashur, having a due regard
to his own skin, had confidently expected.

But, when Jeremiah thought of silence, it was as
a burning fire shut up in his bones. He could no
more be guilty of complicity in his country's ruin
by criminal silence than by lies. He had no wish
to practise self-denial any more than was quite
necessary, but the final, irresistible, compelling
necessity only God's word in his heart could lay
upon him, not any word of man, however enforced
with scourge or stocks. The crowd might surround

him in the day time with mocking word and angry blow and they might leave him in the night to his long pain and his long thoughts, but it was all in vain while a stronger constraint than theirs lay upon his spirit.

Even the longest night at length will pass. With the morning Pashur comes and, of his condescension and good pleasure, orders the prisoner to be taken out of the stocks. Then, as Jeremiah struggles upright on his sore and stiffened limbs, you can see the difference between having fire in one's bones and only healthy lubricating marrow. You see Jeremiah chilled, haggard, weary, with sleepless, burning eyes, and you see Pashur with the red of good living on his cheeks, the glow of sleep warmed from the fleece of his flock, and that sleek and spacious air with which success alone can endow its children.

But, suddenly, all is changed. The authentic high officer of God is Jeremiah. It is now Pashur's turn to sit white and haggard in the stocks. The fire goes from Jeremiah's bones into his eyes and his tongue, and he flashes out on Pashur: 'The Lord hath not called thee Pashur, Prosperity all Round, but Magor-missabib, Terror round About.'

What the Lord had called him had not concerned Pashur much hitherto, but the importance of it now came home to him with the insistence of the very physical force he understood. 'Thus saith the Lord, Behold I will make thee a terror to thyself and to all thy friends.' Before his sight they would

fall by the sword, and he himself would go captive
to Babylon and there be slain; while the gain for
which he had sold his soul would serve only to
tempt the spoiler.

There was something to blanch the red of good
living in his cheek and put a fire of terror in his
bones to replace the fire of God he had so persistently quenched. What the Lord had called him
had come to be, as some day it always must, the
one matter worth any thought. From that time he
could only stagger forward, a terror-stricken wretch,
helpless in the grip of mere physical necessity,
seeing the calamities his profitable lies and com-
pliances had provoked sweep himself and his friends
and all that belonged to them into the abyss.

Then, at length, the difference between the two
kinds of necessity to which a man can subject his
soul can no longer be ignored, for even in that
submerging flood of ruin and desolation and despair,
Jeremiah remained 'a defenced city and an iron
pillar and brazen walls,' the one hope of the stricken
people he had so long warned in vain.

With good success in outward things and health
and manifold activities and attention well fixed
on what man calls us because of our reputation and
standing in the world, the stress of life's tremendous
issues may be long escaped. The notion that life
is a business of taking up our cross daily may be
so remote as not even to seem absurd, or become
the pleasantest unreality, as when one hangs up a

crucifix over the bed whereon his last desire is to suffer God to deal with his heart. But sooner or later everyone's palace of illusion falls about his ears. Then nothing is of any practical concern at all except what God has called him, except, that is to say, what he really is and how it will ultimately fare with him amid the realities God appoints to try his spirit.

By this I am not meaning to say that the good things in your life are wrong in themselves, or that you should not accept them gratefully, or that you should try to bring troubles in their place. But a very smooth life does give cause for asking whether it is of our own appointing or of God's and whether it is concerned only with appearance or with reality. And if you have met no great problems, faced no great decisions, stood in no weakness and perplexity before great duties, and found nothing to pursue more imperative than success, you can be quite sure that you have been governed by no necessity higher than circumstances, and that some day circumstances—if nothing earlier, at least the great circumstance of death—will put it all mercilessly to the test, and that it will no longer be prosperity all round but merely terror round about.

Other things being equal we should all prefer to be Pashur honoured in the chief seat of the temple to Jeremiah dishonoured in its lowest. To make light of ease and honour and prosperity is only another poor unreality. We are not even self-deceived, but are only offering ourselves a very foolish kind

of incense, when we pretend that they have no
value for us. But first be sure that other things
are equal, especially the vital, the victorious, the
impregnable things both for this life and the next.
They are just what God appoints, the truth He
requires you to utter, the deed He requires you to do
and such consequences of them as He requires you
to bear. You have only to prefer what is good to
what merely seems good and leave the rest to
God. Then let your life be as easy and prosperous
as God grants.

To those who already have life's commentary
upon this old story I would say no more, but I
should like to add a word to those whose experience
of life is still to come.

You are entering upon life, setting out to carve
your way in the world. Though you do not whisper
it abroad, you have high hopes and high ambitions.
May you not yet write your name on the roll of
fame? At least the record of your career will surely
be prosperity all round, a success less conspicuous
it may be, but not less comfortably substantial
than you dreamed. In itself that is by no means
wrong. You are not to go to seek trials; you are
not to practise self-denial any more than is quite
necessary.

But then comes the question: What will you
find necessary, what will you find the only way to
true manhood? This at all events you can be sure
of. It will be concerned not with what you seem to

be but with what you are, not with the pleasant and profitable, but with the true and the right. It will be what God appoints for you and not what you appoint for yourself, which, even if it be outwardly smooth, will not be without inward conflict. And the probability is that it will not be smooth either without or within. Look upon Jeremiah in the stocks in the high gate of Benjamin. Look upon a greater than Jeremiah. See Him spit upon, buffeted, nailed to the Cross. For you also that is what the everlasting wisdom and love may appoint.

Your heart sickens at the sight. You turn from it and you say, you will appoint your own life, and, whatever else may be wanting to it, it shall at least be prosperity all round.

But what will that mean? It will mean that you quench the fire of God in your bones. Now the fire of God is a terrible endowment, and if there were nothing beyond what we see, it might be well that it should never be kindled in us, that there should never be anything in our bones but soft lubricating marrow. It is a terrible necessity this, to speak God's word, however unpopular, and do God's will, however unprofitable.

But if it is the bed-rock necessity of life, all the other necessities of chance and circumstance and age and death are at once put in a quite subordinate place. Even this life and this material world can in a quite amazing manner be put under our feet. Nor, without this victory will there be peace, even the poor peace you have chosen, when God's authentic messengers of loss and pain shake your souls and drive you back upon reality.

In the end, though you surrender nothing, the final unavoidable force which strips you of home and friends and kindred and body and breath, will come and ask, what God has called you, and whether you have quenched the fire of God, the immortal flame which burns up to God Himself and without which you are only clay, only of the earth, earthy.

Surrender you must, and the only question is, Under what compulsion? Is it under God's will or only under God's might? In the former case, you will be, even amid the wreck of time and the advent of eternity, 'an iron pillar and brazen walls,' and, in the latter, it will be mere 'terror round about.'

This is the word of the Cross, without which no life is secure either for time or eternity, for though it says, this awful thing may be thy Father's will, it also says, this is the will of pardon, of grace, of wise love, which leads thee to life, by the way of victory, unconquerable strength and never failing peace.

XVII

THE LENGTH AND BREVITY OF LIFE

PSALM lxxiii. 24. 'Thou shalt guide me with thy counsel, and afterward receive me with glory.'

A KEEN sense of the fleeting nature of our mortal life is usually thought to trouble only morbidly religious minds. Sensible people, it is assumed, will relegate the subject to their death-beds. But, to ensure success in this forgetfulness, it is even more necessary to lack imagination than to lack religion.

It is not by accident that, in the Old Testament, the transitoriness of life is set forth in vivid figure and poetic language. To the Wise Woman of Tekoa, we are as water spilt on the ground which cannot be gathered up again; to the Psalmist, we are as grass which flourishes at morning and at even is cut down and withered; to the Prophet, we are as leaves in an autumn wood being whirled down by the wind of our iniquity. These are not the dull platitudes of lugubrious piety, but the imaginative insight of poetic souls. And most memorable and poignant of all are the words of the author of Job, one of the supreme poets of all ages. 'Man that is born of a woman is of few days and full of trouble. He cometh forth as a flower and is cut down: he fleeth also and continueth not!' How often have they been spoken over mortal clay! And how do they stir our hearts afresh with every repetition!

The only passage from all literature which we could put alongside it is that which speaks of the splendour of the world as 'an insubstantial pageant faded,' and of ourselves as 'such stuff as dreams are made on.' And that is by the greatest poet of all, our own Shakespeare. Nor was ever anyone more haunted by the sense of all devouring time, the sense that 'nothing stands but for his scythe to mow.' And the reason was not that he was morbidly religious, but that he was in Milton's words, 'Fancy's child,' or, in his own, 'of imagination all compact.'

What dulls the sense of all things hastening to decay is not wisdom and strength of mind, but routine and forgetfulness. From them faith and imagination alike awake us. And, what is more, they wake us after the same fashion of turning the oblivious round into a wonder and an expectation. Not the mere sense that 'our moments hasten toward their end,' but the vision of time's measureless possibilities makes life seem so short. Till we first realise its greatness, we cannot fully realise its smallness. In a sense it must be long before it is short. What is but 'a vapour which appeareth for a little' is, not the life of a gnat, but the life of a man, in which the small and great are inseparable.

Poetry says to our hearts, 'Thus passes the glory of the world,' by causing us to realise 'what a piece of work is man,' how supreme in faculty, how exalted in interest, how measureless in possibility, how vast in spiritual possessions of truth and beauty, and not by turning our thoughts to the 'bubble reputation' and the tinsel show of place and possession. Similarly religion reveals life's evanescence as a moment between eternities by setting eternity in man's heart. Only its decisions of infinite moment make him realise how fleeting is life's opportunity, and its vision of a city which has foundations how there is here no certain dwelling-place.

Thus, for imagination and faith alike, the sense that life is 'swifter than a weaver's shuttle' depends on seeing the glory of the web it may weave. Especially the sense of the shortness of life is not religious at all, unless we first realise how long it is, measured by the possibilities of good, and still more, by the possibilities of choosing wrong and working evil. Hence our first religious need is security for its length, not its brevity, for achieving its true uses, not for meeting even its near and certain end.

Our first need is SECURITY IN VIEW OF THE LENGTH OF LIFE.

'Thou shalt guide me with thy counsel.'

The need of such security life and his own foolish thoughts about it had taught the Psalmist. He had seen the wicked live in arrogance and die at ease, and he had suffered and seen others suffer under their oppression, till he doubted whether God knew or cared, and whether it was not vain to keep the hands clean and the heart pure.

The old belief that God always gives prosperity to the good and overthrows the wicked was, he knew, not true, so far at least as this life can show. As he believed in another life, we might have expected him to turn to the easy solution that eternity would redress the unjust balance of time. Some have even rested their whole hope of immortality on this seemingly necessary inference from God's righteousness. Yet he did not so much as glance at this facile transference of the problem of God's rule in an unequal world to an unknown future. Nor, what is more, did any prophet.

For that there are at least two good reasons. First, in spite of all the patent injustice of the present, the prophet never ceased to seek to see the 'goodness of the Lord in the land of the living'; and, second, he never ceased to live a life not measured by reward either in time or eternity. In short this solution was not adequate either to his faith or to his morals. Laws enforced by rewards and penalties like a criminal code were not for the prophet the thoughts of God which are as high above our thoughts as the heavens above the earth; nor was doing good for the sake even of everlasting happiness what he understood by God's righteousness. God's thoughts would be like ours in our self-righteous moods, did He measure action by rules and its consequences by a nice apportionment of pleasure and pain: and, if He expected no higher service, the scoff, 'Does Job fear God for nought?' would apply to all without exception. Other-worldliness may be a more prudent foresight, but it has no more purity of motive than worldliness. Man is not truly good, if he does good not for its own sake, but for ulterior reward: and God is not truly good, if He has wholly postponed the principles of His government to the world to come.

When the Psalmist's feet had well nigh slipped through suffering himself to be envious at the prosperity of the wicked, he took another way, and set himself to a better judgment of the life he knew, and not to the application of his old judgment to a life still unknown.

Two things helped him—God's children and God's sanctuary. He looked on good men and knew that to envy the wicked is to betray the cause of the good, for they enjoy a portion they would not exchange for any fortune, power or pride of place. Then he went into the sanctuary and lifted up his heart to God, till the veil was removed from his own soul and he saw man's true blessings through God's large and gracious purpose. Thereupon, all his estimates of life's good were changed, so that he would not have been one of the ungodly to gain the whole world. Then he knew that there was no greater need in life than guidance to choose none of their ways.

Thus he made the great discovery that God's guidance is not by laws which approve themselves by making us prosperous, but by counsel which to accept as our own is itself blessedness.

Laws are externally imposed, and are obeyed, not for their own sake, but for the rewards and punishments attached to them. As positive precepts, they can only insist on obvious duties which can be measured by rule; as prohibitions, they cannot go beyond definite transgressions and patently unclean desires. Laws even of God, though He looks on the heart and not the outward appearance, cannot go further. But counsel we follow only as we make it our own; and we make it our own only as we see it to be in accord with the nature of things as they really are. Yet it is for us good counsel only as we know its wise discernment to be ever beyond us. Thus it is at once positive and measureless in all it proposes to us. Above all, this is true of the counsel of God, which we make our own as it becomes our own judgment of life, yet causes us humbly to realise that life's noblest uses are still beyond our highest imagination and aspiration. The moment our true guidance ceases to be a Judge's law and becomes a Father's counsel, the aims of life at once become higher and greater, yet more secure. God's counsel standeth forever, because it is in accord with the way He has actually made the world and the soul of man to use it, and because it embodies a purpose we never can exhaust.

Yet counsel is counsel only when freely given and freely received. Hence it is possible to 'contemn the counsel of the Most High,' just because it is counsel and not law. But, as it is identical with the nature of God's reality, the rejection of it must be a greater disaster than the breaking of any law. No arbitrarily attached punishment can be so calamitous as to have all God's working necessarily against us. To think otherwise is to live in a dream, which being based on unreality, will be short, and suddenly and terribly broken.

This may at first look as though the Psalmist, when he reached this conclusion, recanted his view that the wicked may die without remorse as well as live without trouble, and that the righteous may have a full cup of bitterness wrung out to them to the very dregs of life. But of these happenings his discovery altered nothing. Only, seeing them with different eyes, he found in them a different meaning.

Possibly he was thinking specially of Jeremiah, the prototype of the Servant of the Lord, a man of sorrows and acquainted with grief, his message despised, his devotion called fanaticism, his sincerity rewarded by the stocks and the lash, his devotion to his people's good restrained in a dungeon. But, though poor, despised, misrepresented, hated, and walking daily with his life in his hand, how was Jeremiah right when others were wrong, how was he loyal when others were false, how was he steadfast when others were dismayed: how was he devoted when others were self-seeking! What treasures of the heart, what peace in the unwavering choice of good, what certainty about life's calls, what service of a man's noblest hopes, what revelation of God's mind, and of the blessed world when He shall have written His counsel on human hearts! What a contrast in security to strutting on the stage of life, dressed in a little brief authority of which death makes mockery, and pampering the body which is to feed the worms!

Our second need is SECURITY IN VIEW OF THE BREVITY OF LIFE.

'And afterward receive me with glory.'

It is often said that there is no trace of any hope of immortality in the early writings of the Old Testament and even that it does not appear at all till after the Exile. We must not, however, assume that at an earlier date the soul was thought to have no continuance, but to suffer dissolution with the body.

The kind of survival now maintained by Spiritualism has always been held by primitive peoples, and the more certainly the more primitive they were. In ancient Israel departed souls were thought to go down to Sheol, which did not mean the grave, but a place in the underworld. There they lived a shadowy existence, where they could not praise God or behold the inhabitants of the world; yet they had knowledge, especially of the future, not given to the living, and could return at times to communicate it, as Samuel to Saul. There were persons who were believed to have familiar spirits just like some in our day, and there was a class who made a profession of appealing to the dead on behalf of the living, who would now be called mediums.

There are people among us who are convinced that, if such a type of continuance after death could be established, a scientific proof of immortality would be provided far more valid than any merely spiritual hope, and that anything the spiritual hope requires could be added afterwards.

But history does not seem to approve this expectation, for, though this kind of belief has been held from time immemorial, no hope of immortality which has anything to do with being received with glory has ever been built on this foundation. To this day it rather appears as if the prophets were right in regarding that kind of interest in the dead as merely a hindrance in 'seeking unto our God' who has appointed our immediate service among the living.

At all events Israel's true hope of immortality came in quite another way. It came by the discovery of a glory in this life, fleeting as it is, vast enough to overflow the bounds of earthly existence, and enduring enough to belong not to time but to eternity. In short, it came entirely through men like Jeremiah who sought nothing whatsoever except to know the counsel of God and to be wholly guided by it. They no more lived for eternal reward than for temporal. But, as they stood for causes which could not perish, were guided by principles which could not alter, and saw visions of a Divine purpose which could not fade, it became unthinkable that, having so lived in things unseen and eternal, they should themselves belong only to things seen and temporal. Like all God's best gifts, the hope of immortality was not found by seeking it, but it came of itself, as our text says, after seeking only to follow God's counsel. 'Thou shalt guide me with thy counsel and afterward,' and only afterward, 'receive me with glory.' There is no meaning to be attached to any conception of eternal glory except as God has guided us on a way which is now eternal. Though we may have to walk in it with bowed back and bleeding feet, it leads us to the mount of vision, where we see, in the humble things of His service, a purpose large enough for the uses of eternity. Only when we have won them by humbly serving them, can we know that the things of truth and beauty and goodness are an unfading glory, to be believed in and hoped for and loved for ever.

Jesus Christ has for us brought life and immortality to light in the good-news, in comparison with which its manifestation, by Jeremiah or even by the whole generation of God's children, is only as the shadow to the sunshine. But, when this is made an isolated matter of the Resurrection, it is no more than the old material basis which had so little value; and it runs counter to our Lord's own saying that neither would men be persuaded though one rose from the dead. The Resurrection is of value as it shows that it was not possible that One who alone walked perfectly in the whole counsel of God should be holden of death.

The emphasis is always on the Cross, which Jesus also conceived as a cup, the full cup into which was wrung out all the bitterness of outward defeat, scorn, ignominy, agony, death, and the sense of being hated of man and even of being forsaken of God. But it was also the supreme fulfilment of all righteousness, because, in face of every pleasure which could bribe or terror which could dismay, and against every counsel of fear or prudence, it marks an utter trust in the counsel of God for guidance in all conceivable circumstances. Not till we see in this perfect service the glory of a love unconquerable in the power of which we too may now live victoriously, can we rest on it a hope for another life in the assurance that neither life nor death can separate us from the love of God which is in Christ Jesus. Nor, without it, can we attach any definite meaning to appearing with Him in glory.

We still know not what we shall be, for God would not have us be distracted from our tasks in this world by the splendour of another, but we know that we shall be like Him, for we shall see Him as He is. When, denying self and taking up our cross and following Christ, we are wholly guided by God's counsel, we learn that the thoughts of God's heart about all He means His children to be and to achieve are not merely for the few moments of our mortal life, but stand to all generations. After we thus have the power of an endless life, and only after that, can we know, with an assurance never to be put to shame, that God will receive us with glory, ministering an abundant entrance into the everlasting Kingdom of our Lord. As we apply the principles of eternity to time, time enlarges for us into the promise of eternity.

XVIII

A MINISTRY OF SORROW

Ezekiel xxiv. 16. 'Son of man, behold, I take away from thee the desire of thine eyes with a stroke.'

This title 'Son of man' is given to Ezekiel alone among all the prophets. Probably we should have judged him the last to deserve it. However much more it may mean, it is a poetical and typical way of addressing him as man. But it is just the large, direct, simple humanity of the other great prophets which we seem to miss in him. His views seem at times limited and formal, and even his morality legal and ceremonial. His passion for justice lacks Micah's democratic fire, his opposition to vice Hosea's pathos, and even his moral indignation comes short of the sublime intensity of Amos. He has nothing of Isaiah's splendour of thought and utterance; and, compared with his contemporary Jeremiah, his insight is less inspired, his sympathy less moving, his appeal less searching. Had it been our selection, would it not of all men have been Jeremiah we should have selected as the type of

> The Human with his droppings of warm tears?

Yet this incident lifts a veil which shows us Ezekiel in an unexpected light, revealing an intimacy of relation to our common human experience of suffering, not possible even for Jeremiah, who had been forbidden to involve himself in social ties. The day of disaster found Jeremiah stronger because of his solitary state, but it found Ezekiel more deeply involved in all his people's sufferings, so that, if Jeremiah's were the diviner position, Ezekiel's was the more human.

This story of how Ezekiel had to meet personal and public calamity may be taken as covering three days, which mark three stages of the transformation of human sorrow into faith and peace.

The first is a day of a sentence of death which was far more terrible to him than if it had been passed upon himself, and of pleading with his people while he stood himself in the shadow of this doom. With the tender earnestness and passionate insistence of his own impending calamity, he offered his hearers, for the last time, the way of penitence as an escape from theirs.

The word of the Lord had come to him saying, 'Son of man, behold, I take away from thee the desire of thine eyes with a stroke.' With that burden on his heart he spoke to the people in the morning, and at even his wife died.

This one poetic word, 'the desire of thine eyes,' shows with a flash what fire was in the flint, what romance in the outwardly stern and even formal man. The true man appears, as when, under the cunning and grasping of Jacob which seemed void of the possibility of passion, we learn there was a love for Rachel which made the seven years he served for her seem but a few days.

Ezekiel in public was a mere stern incarnate accusing conscience. Before his people and in fulfilment of his mission to call men to repentance, God had made his 'face hard against their faces and as an adamant harder than flint had He made his forehead.' Yet while there was in him this side 'to face the world with,' there was another 'to show a woman when he loved her.' When we understand this, we read all his life with a difference. We see here, too, that God reveals Himself by needing the most tender-hearted of his children for His sternest tasks, because mere hardness has no edge of steel unless it has been tempered in the fire of great pity and love. We understand, too, the difficulty of his call, how the hand of the Lord had to be strong upon him before he could be brought to enter upon a life of relentless conflict with imperturbable impenitence, and how, when he left his home in Palestine to carry his message to the captives in Mesopotamia, he went in 'bitterness, in the heat of his spirit.'

There, in face of venomous hatred and in utter loneliness, he entered upon those strange, long symbolic warnings which made such exhausting demands both upon the flesh and upon the spirit. But his wife was a true help-mate. Her love found some way of making that long hard journey; and one day she came to him with the glory of a love-light in her eyes, such as he had never seen even on the day of their first espousals. His mission still made no progress, his message stirred no less hatred, the opposition was no less bitter, but all was changed when at home he had the sunshine of perfect sympathy and perfect understanding.

Now that dear face was to be hid in 'death's dateless night,' and life for him would be almost as dateless as death, one long companionless and desolate day, without any screen from the keen edged winds of man's ingratitude and hate, and with a great emptiness in his heart, which would make all that happened to him from without mere things indifferent.

Yet she had one day still of earthly ministry, and surely her greatest. You cannot suppose that such a shadow on her beloved's soul could be hidden from the keen eyes that had been accustomed to read his inmost thoughts; nor can you suppose that, when she knew, her thought was for herself. No doubt her thought was of the lonely man she must leave to travel uncomforted the waste places of life, yet not as though, either for her sake or his own, she could conceive him neglecting his duty. The woman who could be the light of a prophet's eyes, must have had something of the immortal strain of fire and spirit in her love. Must we not conceive her with the quality of John Welsh's wife, who could beg on her knees that her husband's life might be saved by restoration to his native air, but who held out her apron and said, 'I would rather

kep' his head there,' when she heard that the condition
was that he should recant.

As unselfishly as Ezekiel himself she must have
dedicated the last day they would spend together to
his task, so that he could go forth equipped by her
sympathy to make his last appeal.

The shadow both of private and public calamity
lay black upon his spirit, yet surely God enabled
him that morning to appeal with more than the old
intensity and inflexible courage and grave emphasis
and fearful insistence. There would be also a new
and trembling passion of tender sympathy and gentle
patience and personal pity, without which he could
not have rightly said that God had fully spoken
through him to the obdurate hearts of his brethren.
As he realised how the last grains of opportunity
were running in the glass both for them and for
him, his face would be no more hard, his brow
no longer adamant, his message no more a mere
death-sentence, his audience no more a rebellious
people. Something of the personal quality of the
divine omniscience would be granted him, which
could feel what every soul before him would suffer
when the sun of hope finally set upon a dying world.
This would work in his hitherto merely stern message
such a transformation as when the warm, soft but
mighty flame breaks out of the hard black coal,
such a transformation as took place when our Lord
passed from 'Woe unto you, Scribes and Pharisees,
hypocrites,' to 'O Jerusalem, Jerusalem...Behold,

your house is left unto you desolate.' Men would hear in it a new and more appealing note, a note perhaps only to be rightly struck by those who stand in the shadow both of personal sorrow and public calamity.

That was the task of the morning. The afternoon God would give him, from regard to his human affection. No doubt he told his wife what he had done, and received a smile of approval which assured him that their duty and affection would be eternally intertwined.

And then those dear eyes never shone upon him again on earth. With the gathering shadows of evening the stroke fell. Prepare for it as we may, we never realise what a stroke is till it does fall. No certainty of approaching bereavement ever quite prepares the heart for the blankness of the vacant place, for the cold, dreary emptiness of the world, for the poor, dazed groping of the dismayed heart. In the long hours of that solitary night Ezekiel drained his cup of sorrow, realising, in all its vivid reality, how his house was left to him desolate, and that desolate his heart would be all the days which remained of his earthly pilgrimage.

The second day had an even harder task in store for him, a task to which his night's experience had given individual, personal, appalling meaning. It was a task to swallow up the thought of his great personal loss; or, if he could not but think of it, to reconcile him to it. Though never in his life, hard as it had been, had he stood so much in need of sympathy and comfort, he knew that the work before him needed a lonely spirit, and that it was of God's great mercy that the tender heart of a woman had been spared the agony of such a day.

'And I did in the morning,' he says, 'as I was commanded.' In his gay clothes, dry-eyed, without token or sign of grief, he went and stood in the public way. God did not ask him to volunteer his message. That would have been too terrible. He must wait till a scandalised public demanded the meaning of his unseemly conduct. Then he was to tell a story which would freeze the warm blood in the heart.

Jerusalem was about to fall, and everything they honoured and everyone they loved to go down in the ruin. God would profane His sanctuary, the excellency of His people's strength, the desire of their eyes; and in the slaughter their sons and daughters would perish. Nothing would remain of the worship and the homes, the hope of returning to which had alone sustained their hearts all the days of their exile in that alien and inhospitable land. When all alike are desolate and hopeless, mourning is choked in the utterance, and all symbols of grief become mockery. Heedless of outward forms, dry-eyed, and with mere moaning toward one another, as all the expression they could compass, they would pine away in their sin-stricken souls.

It was an appalling judgment, and, in other days,

it would have been delivered with appalling sternness. But on this day Ezekiel in his bereavement, his tenderness, his resignation, his humble sincerity, was a sign to that stricken people of another quality. Death and desolation were to him no longer mere well-deserved judgments of a righteous God. But, his indignation being softened to pity, he knew it as the agony of individual souls, the greater that they were weak and sinful. This compassion taught men, as condemnation had never done, that only in loving-kindness does God appoint sorrow to follow sin, and thereby softened them to penitence and encouraged them to hope.

To-day still there are among us men and women like Ezekiel from whom God has removed the light of their eyes with a stroke, who go out in the morning and wait at their old places, sad-eyed and patient, for us to ask what it means. And when we ask, they say to us the same things. The light of our eyes shall be taken away and our homes desolate and what we hold sacred profaned and our possessions turned to ashes and the things in which we trusted crumbled to dust. Then we shall have lost in time what we might have won for eternity, if for love we chose lust, for duty pleasure, for goodness gain, for God the fashion of this world that passes away. They speak no longer in mere judgment, as if sin were gain could we only escape punishment, but in understanding and compassion and tender pity for our waste of life's most precious gifts and our desolating neglect of life's great opportunity. Such individual discernment and fellow-feeling few possess without experience of sorrow as well as of conflict. But, without it, no one can reveal to another the true disaster of sin or touch the heart to real penitence.

Yet not till the third day did the true meaning of his experience clearly dawn upon the prophet. Hitherto he had seen no fruit of all his labours. Whether men heard or whether they forbore, he had faithfully delivered God's warning; and, at least till he spoke out of his own sorrow, they would not hearken. But as he watched beside his dead, bitterness passed from him, the heat of his spirit died down, and rebellion was turned to gratitude that his beloved was delivered from the day of evil. Yet he still felt in his desolation the hand of the Lord heavy upon him. But as he sat alone through the dark watches of another night, God gave back to him, purified and made perfect, all he had lost.

Other earthly things might be dust, but he now knew that a partnership, fashioned by the spirit of duty in the fire of love, death cannot dissolve; and what is stronger than death he knew could only be of God. There was no blundering with our human affections. Had not God Himself called his wife, 'the light of his eyes'? God had taken nothing without knowing the cost. Then Ezekiel knew, in a sense he never knew before, that God is the Lord, the Lord even of these appalling disasters, the Lord of life and death no doubt, but with love, and not merely judgment, controlling all destinies.

That God wills not the death of the sinner but would rather men came to Him and lived, he had always known and declared. But now something came home to him of the supreme revelation that a merciful wisdom works in all events—and not least in the most terrible—seeking and saving the lost.

In the day when God took away the desires of men's eyes and all whereon they set their hearts—strength, renown, possession, kindred, when all others were dumb, his mouth would be opened, and he would be a sign, not only of holy living and meek resignation, but of confident hope that God is Lord over this and all events for the ends of a love which could never leave us in sin, but also could never leave us in despair.

For each one of us too, in days of sorrow and bereavement, there is consolation in that Divine word, 'The light of thine eyes.' There is no endearing name we can bestow upon our kindred and our friends but God also calls them by, and there is no bereavement without His knowing all it means to us of empty homes and desolate hearts.

In God's sight even the vastest upheavals are no mere deciding of the destiny of nations, but His measure, as ours ought to be, ay, and His meaning, as ours ought to be, is concerned with the agony of human hearts. This is the real scorching fire of the discipline. But it is also the true hope of purification and peace. Only as that human experience concerns us and we see in it matters of eternal moment, and realise that the external things whereon men set their hearts are, in any case, dust and ashes, can our mouths be opened to make men know that God is still the Lord, with all destinies in His hand, and that He determines all events for His one supreme treasure upon earth—the soul of man that lives by duty and by love. For it still the Lord God Omnipotent reigneth.

XIX

STRENGTH THROUGH WEAKNESS

Acts xiv. 19. 'And having persuaded the crowds, these stoned Paul, and dragged him out of the city, thinking him to be dead.'

In the course of his hazardous life Paul suffered many persecutions, yet this stoning at Lystra stands out by itself. No other left him as dead, and it would appear that he suffered from it permanent bodily injury. But the deep impression it left on his mind was due still more to the experiences which followed it and their effect upon the whole course of his ministry.

This we gather chiefly from the Epistle to the Galatians. Our right to use that Epistle in this connection depends on the view that it was written to the group of churches in which Lystra was included. This, I admit, is still questioned by good authorities, but not, I think, for good reasons. In any case, my interpretation of the incident depends on regarding 'the former visit' when he preached 'because of an infirmity of the flesh,' which is mentioned in Galatians, as taking place on the return journey from Derbe to Antioch after this persecution, the 'former' distinguishing it from the 'first' on the journey forward.

That the infirmity was not disease, but permenent

injuries from persecution, appears from the description of it as the stigmata or owner's marks of the Lord Jesus. The natural interpretation is that the suffering and weakness, which followed the assault, forced Paul and his companions to alter their plan and return by the way they came. The former visit, when he preached through infirmity, would then be intentionally distinguished from the first visit when he appeared in the fullness of his vigour.

When he says, some years after, that he still bore in his body the marks of the Lord Jesus, he must have meant that his injuries were both grave and permanent, but, unless he had regarded them as also having wrought some deep and lasting spiritual change, he would not have referred them so solemnly to the Lord Jesus. That spiritual change may be summed up in his own words. He learned that when he was weak, then he was strong. It was one experience, but his whole later experience was determined by three particular applications of it— the first was to himself, the second to his method, and the third to his gospel. These are the matters of chief importance for us; and we shall consider them in this order.

In the first place, then, IT REVEALED TO PAUL HIS TRUE SELF.

A mechanical idea of inspiration causing them to read his Epistles, which are intimate personal letters, as doctrinal treatises dictated to him from above, has, for many, utterly obscured the humanity of the Apostle. All know his struggles with others, but few discern the intensity of his struggle with himself.

Were he still alive, he might startle his readers, as he did the idolaters at Lystra, by springing forth among them and rending his garments and declaring himself a man of like passions with themselves. He never found the higher faith bring the higher life without struggle and conflict. To the end he did not regard himself as having attained the goal he strove for; and neither nature nor grace ever set him above temptation or above mistake.

In Paul, as in us, there were two men. And, like us too, he sometimes failed to distinguish them. The natural man had great qualities; and, as he speaks of being consecrated to his task from his mother's womb, he manifestly did not regard them as merely evil. He was a man of warm affections and possibly of quick temper. Intellectually he loved subtleties and excelled in debate. He set aside the wisdom of words, but as one who had known its temptation. On occasion he could use the glittering weapon of rhetoric; and he had a subtle understanding of what was persuasive to his audience. A difficult problem always awoke his interest; and he was easy to draw into the mazes of theology. He was a born pioneer; and he was ambitious to succeed in what he undertook. Almost the only tradition of him which may be authentic speaks of his personal magnetism over all he met, in striking contrast to the first effect of his personal appearance. Even from Acts we gather the impression of a man who never failed to rouse violent opposition where he failed to win the most devoted friendship; and the frequency with which he wrought mighty works, that is, miraculous cures, itself proves a dominating influence upon the minds of men. Finally, he was capable of embracing the whole civilised world in his purpose, and of forming a great and consistent plan for carrying it into effect.

If you read the account of his work and his speeches, you will see that, up to this point, this was the man who was constantly in evidence. He is the chief speaker, and his speeches are mainly debate, though at times, as in his appeal to the idolators, he could rise to noble heights of eloquence. His fearless personality never failed to impress, if only to opposition, and his direct influence upon certain minds had sometimes the most amazing effect. His speech and bearing and working made men think him and Barnabas gods, which at least speaks of an extraordinary quality and power.

Men saw a brilliant and successful leader of a new movement, but the new man in Christ Jesus, to whom all things had become new by a great gentleness and patience and loving-kindness, was obscured to the world, and even to his disciples, and perhaps even to himself. The vehemence of his protest, when he was mistaken for a god, may speak of a commotion in his own soul, caused by a glimpse into the abyss of his own thoughts, as well as by reprobation of the idolatry.

The next day taught him the worthlessness of this domination. The man who yesterday was hailed as a god, was to-day stoned like a dog and flung outside the city wall like dead carrion. He came back to consciousness, but it was to the consciousness of being a different person. The broken man who was helped away was no longer one who loved the arena, overwhelmed in debate, bore down opposition by his moral vehemence, and dominated by his spiritual energy. No wonder that he feared the effect upon his converts, and dreaded to be despised and rejected.

But a new man appeared who was a new manifestation of Christ, whom his converts received, not, according to his fears, as a pretender circumstances had unmasked, but as a messenger of God, even as Jesus Himself.

That was the heart of the whole matter. The Galatians saw Christ in him; they learned, as no eloquence or miracle could teach them, what it meant to be a Christian. They learned that true strength and victory was of gentleness and patience, and they discerned a spirit, which, by turning evil to good, was more than conqueror over all earthly ills. They saw, in short, the man for whom eloquence was sounding brass, and prophecy and miracles and martyrdom profitless without love. And, as this won all hearts, he had surely a right to glory in his afflictions.

Paul's experience is not very different from human experience generally. The more obstreperous the applause, the more suddenly it can turn into hissing and fury. It is the destiny of all human idols one day to be flung out as dead. And, even in our quiet places and among our friends, we are successful to-day and fail to-morrow, are full of health and energy to-day and broken men tottering to the grave to-morrow. Our lease is at will, and the strongest of us cannot contest its terms; and so many hold it with such disabilities that it seems scarce worth retaining. Shattered frames, frustrated hopes, broken minds, desolate hearts require some great good to justify life. But, if we know our souls to be our true good, we have discovered what is worth the price. Our deeper, tenderer, humbler, truer selves too often become encrusted with vanity and domineering and love of possession and place when we have nothing but health and success and ease and approbation. God, in His goodness may have to recall us to our true selves by disease and pain and disaster and bereavement, and not realise for us our earthly desires in a way to make lean our souls.

If any object has commanded the reverence of our generation it is efficiency, the efficiency of health, vigour, mental resource, confidence, organising talent, commanding influence which commands success. But is there not a deeper, more lasting efficiency, with power over the hearts and not merely the bodies of men, having in it the might to make

all things new, only to be won by the weakness
which reveals to us a strength not to be crushed
by all the brute forces of the world? Is not the
truly efficient person, in the end, the new man
in Christ Jesus, pitiful and gentle and kind, who
knows how to bear all things, believe all things,
hope all things, endure all things, and who thereby
turns evil into good, and defeat into victory, and all
the uncertainties of life into the unchanging purpose
of God?

In the second place, IT REVEALED TO PAUL HIS
TRUE METHOD.

We have already seen something of his original
method. If we look at the narrative a little more
closely, we also see the plan on which he meant to
carry it through. The mission had begun in Cyprus,
the native country of Barnabas. From the direction
of their journey, it was apparently meant to end in
Cilicia, the native country of Paul. It was characteristic
of their courage, or rather of their faith, thus to face
first those who knew them best.

At Lystra Cilicia was not far away, but the journey
through the mountains was impossible for a broken
man. One cannot be stoned by an infuriated mob
and flung out as dead without serious injuries.
Paul does not say much about them, but what he
says is full of meaning. His converts, he declares,
would have been ready to pluck out their eyes and
give them to him. The inference is that he was
subject to at least attacks of blindness. He further

describes his infirmity as of a nature his converts might have been tempted to despise or spit out. That seems to indicate attacks of an epileptic type, it being an ancient custom to spit as a means of averting from the spectator the evil spirit which was thought to cause them. Such blinding attacks could easily be caused by a lesion which made him at first seem to be dead. As such fits are often accompanied by violent pain, they may also have been what Paul afterwards described as his 'stake in the flesh.'

The Paul who returned was in no danger of being mistaken for a god. There could be no more debates in the synagogues, no more eloquent appeals, no more publicity of any kind. Between the times Paul spent in pain and Barnabas in care of him, they devoted themselves privately to their converts. We read that they confirmed the souls of the brethren, exhorted them to continue in the faith, appointed elders in every church, and prayed with fasting, commending them to the Lord on whom they had believed. But, then, for the first time, we also read, they made many disciples and could begin to speak of the conversion of the Gentiles. This was the triumph of a new method, more quiet, more personal, more simply religious.

Paul, it is true, did not abandon the old, when he found it useful. He could still argue, when argument was called for; he could still stir up a whole city by his appeals, when commotion was necessary; he was not afraid to exhort, publicly as well as privately, even so seemingly hopeless a subject as a corrupt Roman Governor; he could employ the arts of appeal, even in face of the conceit of wisdom of an Athenian audience. Nor did he ever try without putting all his mind and heart into the task. He never accepted failure, if, by any skill or earnestness, he could succeed.

But it was perhaps in those days when he bore so painfully in his body what he calls the owner's marks of the Lord Jesus, that he formed the habit of mind, which made him afterwards so constantly describe himself as the slave of Jesus Christ, and consider himself every other person's slave for His sake. And a like effect of his weakness appeared in his new method.

In intimate intercourse, in the exchange of hopes and fears, in the quiet influence of faith upon faith and character upon character, in fellowship and united prayer, in discovering those who could guide and teach and create a spirit of mutual trust and helpfulness, in forming small societies to be a leaven of the Kingdom of God in the great world of heathenism, he found the true method of service into which he was henceforth to pour the whole wealth of his nature. It was a lowly service compared with the enticing words of man's wisdom, but it approved itself in demonstration of the spirit and of power.

If the call should come to us, we too may not

shrink from the way of argument and public appeal and affirmation of our convictions, but must follow it with such courage and success as our faith and spiritual power make possible for us. We too must face the charge of being among those who turn the world upside down, should our day demand that of us. And we must go forward with a high heart, putting all our loyalty, all our skill, all our resources into the task. Especially we must stake all our faith, not only in God, but, through God, in man. In the worst there are elements of the best. In the spiritual sphere there is nothing impossible. As each one is a child of God, on behalf of truth and righteousness and the beauty of holiness the last word is neither with us nor with him, but with God.

Yet our true hope of amending the world is in another method, the method of being the servant of Christ in the service of all men.

In these noisy days we are not learning it well; and, in consequence, we are merely dismayed when argument and oratory and well engineered plans and vast organised efforts turn out futilities. The public doings, in which we trusted, are cast out as dead, and we are slow to perceive that a humbler but greater power may rise in their stead. Nor will anything really transforming happen till we win our strength out of weakness, finding it simply in living humbly and hopefully among our fellowmen, so that they cannot doubt that we are messengers of God, or fail to see in us Jesus Christ. Then we shall know that there is no higher or mightier way than to have prayer and fellowship in Christ's name, to seek our natural leaders among those who are inspired by His spirit, and to live humbly for the service of others in His power.

There is an Indian doctrine called *yoga* which means that no one can really teach another person religion. All he can do is to live his own religion, when, in fellowship with him, other people will discover their own religion. Of no religion is this truer than the faith of Christ. We come to Him, not as we are taught of man, but only as we are taught of God. Yet we receive Christ by receiving His brethren, and men can discover Him for themselves only as they see Him in those who are like Him. The greatest work for Christ, therefore, is neither what we say nor what we do, but simply what we are.

In the third place, IT REVEALED TO PAUL HIS TRUE GOSPEL.

The new man is himself the true method, and the new method is itself the true gospel. The essence of it is that, when we are weak in ourselves, then are we strong in God, that, when we discover the worthlessness of the world for our own dominion, we discover its value for God's Kingdom.

Even in his most argumentative speeches Paul aimed at true faith and never at mere intellectual refutation. But his earlier speeches could at the most have produced intellectual conviction. They tended to increase the danger of Christianity becoming merely one of the many movements of thought which, at that time, were causing great commotion, but effecting little spiritual change.

Even when Paul spoke of the Crucifixion, men would not necessarily discern that it was a new view of God and of life and of the true uses of the world. They could still have thought of it as a mere momentary triumph of wickedness in the midst of a revelation of might and glory, with its meaning the assurance that such moments do not last for ever.

But, in his suffering and weakness, Paul struck a deeper note. The faith in which his disciples were exhorted to continue could no longer be mistaken for faith in a glorious triumph of Divine power, but was now, beyond all possibility of misunderstanding, faith in a Kingdom only to be entered through much tribulation.

No doubt he was first thinking of persecutions. He had seen that there was nothing worth maintaining in the world which the world would not condemn. And were we truer to our highest insight and noblest convictions, we also would learn the same truth through experience of opposition. Did we commend ourselves more unmistakably to men's consciences, we should more certainly disturb their conventions and be more in conflict with their prejudices and desires. We find life easy and unopposed only because we obscure some of our principles and compromise with others.

But in the days when Paul's plan had been set aside and his activities restricted, when he did nothing without pain and was much driven in upon himself, tribulation came to have a wider meaning and taking up his cross a deeper significance. He learned that no eternal good can be won out of ease of mind and comfort of body and the world's successes and gratifications, and that we find our best only when we go a lonely, difficult way in search of it, and seldom discover God's purpose till our own is frustrated. Then he knew that the Cross of Christ is the eternal meaning of a Kingdom which is a righteousness that is not mere well-doing, a peace that is not mere ease, a joy that is not mere fleeting pleasure.

Though the world is only for the manifestation of God's Kingdom, His Kingdom is not of this world. Hence it is in the nature of things, and not merely by arbitrary Divine appointment, that, to have eternal gain, we must suffer temporal loss. To save us from making this present fleeting world our kingdom, we must suffer disappointment with it at every turn. As the true purpose and blessedness even of this world lie beyond it, we may never hope to find them in it. Wherefore the Cross of Christ is not a mere incident in history, but is the eternal way of every victory in which the spirit triumphs over the flesh.

In these days of concentrated interest in the kingdoms of this world, our vision of that kingdom of the spirit has not been growing clearer. Yet, if we did not see it in the storm of battle, it was because we had already lost it in the sunshine of prosperity. That men should make any sacrifice for the things of the spirit was almost beginning to be thought unnecessary and even incredible. Material success was regarded as ample justification of all ways of living. That our best success might require material failure would have seemed mere preposterous folly.

When we have had time rightly to feel our losses, we may better discern our gains. The immediate call is for our own learning, as we behold the wreck of vast schemes of ambition, the fields of the slain, the worthlessness of human trusts, the destruction of cherished possessions, and look forward to a disturbed and impoverished age. Unless we have a Gospel which can accept tribulation and find it the way into an everlasting kingdom, in what have we hope?

Yet to what are we turning? For the moment at least more than ever to pleasure and gain, and place and power.

The realities of life, however, do not change. The Cross of Christ is still their sole interpretation. We truly gain the world only as, through it, the world is crucified to us and we to the world. The price of the highest must be paid, and it is opposition, and condemnation, and poor success, and stress of thought and aspiration, and inward conflict, and the patience of faith and the service of love.

We have no need to seek trials of our own making, we have no right to fail in any enterprise through our own discouragement or slackness, but we may not escape trial by taking an easy road or secure success by aiming low. The difficult road and the high aim alone lead into the Kingdom, and, as none of its good is in this world, the fashion and lust of which pass away, we can be strong only by what teaches us our own weakness, and we may best succeed by what is for our own purposes failure and disaster.

XX

THE FELLOWSHIP AND THE GOSPEL

PHILIPPIANS i. 3, 5. 'I thank my God with joy...for your fellowship in furtherance of the gospel.'

OUR watch-words for furthering any cause are 'enthusiasm' and 'organisation'; Paul's are 'joy' and 'fellowship.' In this difference lies the secret both of his own amazing devotion to the Gospel and of his faith in these poor, ignorant, imperfect fellow-workers of his as the adequate means for furthering it. To the great organised religions around, religions sanctioned by immemorial custom, housed in vast temples and embodied in impressive rites, with the power of a state behind them to fall back upon which was universal, strong and ruthless, these Christian fellowships were foolish, weak, base, despised, nay, did not exist at all. Yet Paul believed them able to bring to naught even those things which so confidently and mightily were.

Only because he trusted a quite different order of power was such confidence possible. Christianity was of less account than any other religion of the time either for stirring up enthusiasm to a passion or for showing an imposing front. But its followers had in them the breath of life, without which the mightiest institutions decay. Paul speaks of it as wisdom and righteousness and sanctification and redemption. Those who possess it are saints, holy and beloved, heirs of God and joint-heirs, not with himself alone, but with Jesus Christ. Their gatherings represent God's Kingdom upon earth, because each may be filled with knowledge of His will.

The frequency with which he must correct the crudeness of their spiritual ideas and expose the stains upon their moral purity might give the impression of exaltation and unreality to his words, were it not that all his relations with them are on this high plane, so that he never tries to correct an error except by their own discernment of the highest or remove an evil except by appeal to their own loyalty to the noblest. Though he had no illusions either about their ignorance or their weakness, nothing they ever thought or did shook his confidence of something there in the hearts of these people of joyful possession of God's truth to which appeal could be made, and of power whereby the victory which alone is truly moral, the triumph of one's own soul over evil, could be won.

More especially Paul was confident that this common possession of God's good-news now, with its gift of peace and hope, and its promise of a new humanity in a new earth and a new heaven in the years to come, was itself sufficient to give them the closest unity, which he calls fellowship. Nor is anything in his life more deserving of note than the absence of every effort to promote co-operation except by awaking this sense of joy in possessing a common good.

The very idea of fellowship is inward spiritual relation: and with this meaning the word is used in the New Testament with a frequency and an almost technical precision which the English translation only imperfectly conveys. Partly, the word fellowship has come in our language to mean little more than association; and, partly, the translators, influenced by this fact, substituted communion in what they regarded as more solemn connections. But fellowship in the Early Church was always in the most solemn connection. It expressed the essential Christian relation to each other. To continue in the fellowship was the mark of a true believer, and the chief rite, the breaking of bread, was its seal and manifestation. This was so among themselves, moreover, because fellowship was also the essential relation of God's reconciled children to Himself, the 'fellowship of the Spirit' being their central religious experience. On this relation, which had been produced and maintained by the Gospel, Paul placed all his hopes for furthering the Gospel.

The effect even of an intense belief is not always either direct or simple, but it almost always involves disbelief in something else. When you believe yourself well and vigorous by reason of your own constitution, you do not seek the same result by medicine; when you believe that the rain will abundantly water your field, you do not build irrigation dams; when you think a truth is abundantly proved by reason, you do not enforce it by law and penalties; when you believe men are taught of God, you do not wish to regulate their faith and actions by what you think proper. After this fashion Paul proved his faith in the Christian fellowship. He committed his trust to it so utterly that he took no account of the usual safeguards of organised societies.

His first conviction concerned fellowship in the truth. All he said and did and, still more, all he left unsaid and undone, in his relations with these humble believers shows how sure was his conviction that they had each of them seen for themselves the same truth, and must, therefore, be one in faith.

Converts from heathenism in Paul's time were just like converts from heathenism in our time. They only imperfectly cast off their old views, and the deepest things of the Christian faith they only imperfectly understood. And they had fewer means to help them. The Gentile believers had no sacred writing. The Hebrew had the Old Testament, but they had been trained to read it with rabbinical spectacles. Of the New Testament only a few of the epistles had been written; and they were still read merely as private letters. The only source of instruction was the preaching and conversation of occasional itinerant teachers, which must have been central but could not have been systematic. There was no form of creed. What we call the Apostles' Creed was not in its first form really a creed, and no Apostle had anything to do with it. Why for these small communities, brought up in paganism and still living in an atmosphere of pagan thinking, were not effective outward helps devised for their better instruction in the truth of Christianity?

We can imagine the other Apostles continuing as simple evangelists, merely because they failed to realise the need, but that is an explanation impossible in the case of the theological and organising mind of Paul. If he abstained, it must have been from the sense of having a better method at his disposal.

What he did rely on his writings make evident. His whole appeal was to a truth his readers had seen in Jesus Christ for themselves, which they knew to be of God and not man because it had delivered their souls from superstitions and fears, and set them free in peace and joy, and delivered them from the might of evil, and made the world for them a new creation. To awaking in them an understanding of the full meaning and power of what was already theirs, Paul, therefore, devoted all his powers of persuasion, and he did not dream of imposing it upon them from without by any creed or formula. Instead he urges them to exercise the discernment of spiritual men who can judge all things aright just because they have a truth which delivers them from dependence on any human opinion.

This was very far from assuring the absence of all difference of view. There were differences which even threatened division, and which grieved him to the heart. But he never sought to overcome them by laying down forms upon which to agree. He merely pointed anew to Jesus Christ, as though no return to unity were of any value which was not a common vision of the same reality.

Nor was that all. The one certain development in his mind was an increasing toleration regarding individual and even national differences in conceiving every form of truth. To the Galatians he said, 'If ye are circumcised, Christ profiteth you nothing.' To the Corinthians, a little later, he could say, 'If any man is circumcised, let him not be uncircumcised.' In this epistle to the Philippians, after a few years more, he still urges his readers to be of one mind, but, while he would be glad to have them agreed on one view, he lays all the stress on being of kindred soul. Even on a vital issue of what might seem plain ethical moment, he is prepared to wait for agreement till it come of God's own revealing. Upon this truth of God's own revealing and man's own seeing he placed all his faith for the furthering of the good-news; and he gave thanks for it with joy, just because he knew that no difference arising from human limitation or imperfection in conceiving it could ever deny the essential unity of those who possessed it, or hinder God in revealing His own mind to them in ever fuller, and, therefore, more perfectly uniting measure.

If unity in truth, because all its members see the same reality of God's own manifesting, is the tap-root of fellowship, which gives it strength and stability, the fibres which nourish it and keep it ever green are the loyalties and sympathies and forbearances which come from what the Apostle describes as having the same love, and being of united soul. He finds no figure interdependent enough to express the closeness of this relation except the members of one body: nor is any figure living and close enough for what maintains it except that the head of every one is Christ.

When we are tempted to think his language too exalted for human nature, we should recall how this spirit manifested itself in the days before Christ's revelation of the Father had been enfeebled by admixture with the spirit of the world. For a time it obliterated all sense of private property, and later Paul was able to speak of the help given to the poorer brethren at Jerusalem, not as 'liberality,' as it is translated, but as 'the expression of fellowship.'

A power which could break down what the Apostle calls 'the middle-wall of partition,' the alienation, in the name of religion, between Jew and Greek, might justify the utmost exaltation of language. But still greater was the transformation of human relations by the Gospel which made Mary the mother of Jesus and Mary Magdalene sisters, Simon the zealot and Matthew the publican fellow-apostles, Paul the learned Jewish rabbi and Onesimus the runaway Gentile slave father and son. Was it not good ground for believing that a power from God Himself had come into the world equal to the task both of regenerating our present society and of assuring the promise of a greater heavenly society beyond it?

Like everything else on earth, it had its conflict with the divisive forces of human nature and human society. Nor were any of them absent from these Christian communities. Our distinctions—rank, possession, reputation, education—were there, and, in addition, distance was less easily bridged, languages were less easily translated, and religion still more openly reinforced national hatreds. Occasional grave failures the Apostle makes no attempt to conceal. More especially it appeared in misuse of the ordinance which was the very symbol and bond of brotherhood. Though the essence of the Lord's Supper was to be one bread, one body, it was made the occasion for displaying abundance and forgetting need. Some were drunken and others hungry: and it is characteristic of Paul's judgment that he seems to have felt the hunger, even more than the drunkenness, to be a denial of all the ordinance signified.

But most to be noted is his indifference to the abuses, and his concentration upon the absence of

the spirit of brotherhood which should have pre-
vented them. Nothing could have been easier than
to lay down a form of observance which would
at once have removed all unseemliness. But he
knew that, in spite of every pagan element which
survived, there was in the heart of these people a
spirit whereby a unity far greater in itself and far
mightier in furthering the Gospel of love could be
realised than was possible for the best outward
ordering. Believing it, moreover, to be, not of
man's organising, but of God's implanting, he did
nothing whatsoever except appeal to it. For one
who had lifted up his heart to God in joy and
gratitude for the bond of the spirit of Jesus and the
love of the Father with His brethren, mere ruling
out differences and imposing uniform names and
arranging visible bonds could only seem a human,
temporary and imperfect way of uniting God's
children.

Many would have said, How do all these visible
abuses hinder the Gospel! and have set themselves,
by every means at their disposal, to suppress them.
But the Apostle knew that the only real hindrance
to the Gospel was the absence of the spirit of the
Gospel, and, therefore, he gave all his strength to
awaking it. In one word his faith was in fellowship,
not organisation: and a fellowship is distinguished
from an organisation by being dependent, not upon
visible uniformities, but upon a spirit of understanding, sympathy, patience and personal affec-

tion, in which men are not alienated because they differ.

Finally, something more is necessary for growth than tap-root and fibres. They produce nothing without the coming of the spring. But the Gospel was for the Apostle just the call of the spring, the rising of the sun above the storms and clouds of earth, which makes each one who lives under its influence, in his own way, put forth the special vital forces which God has implanted in him, so that the earth clothes itself in verdure and becomes a harmony of varied and abundant promise.

The Gospel concerned nothing less than the Rule of the God and Father of our Lord Jesus Christ, a Rule by Christ's method and for the ends He manifested. The Gospel to be furthered was this good-news of the Kingdom: and the fellowship furthered it by being a colony, an outpost of it in the world. All its members were one in this service, not by visible arrangement, but by being, in the inmost loyalty of their hearts, citizens of it.

At first sight this faith in the Kingdom of the Father might seem less prominent in the teaching of the Apostle than in the teaching of his Master. But when he speaks of being 'in Christ' he means being in the world in which Christ lived, the world where, being reconciled to the Father, we find His will the purpose of goodness for which all things work and by which all experience is re-created for us by love and wisdom, in a world of new men and new values, and therefore of new securities both for time and eternity.

But the highest evidence of his faith in this Kingdom of God is his way of treating even the most imperfect believers as citizens of it. He has often to warn them even against gross sins, but he carefully refrains from anything like legal prohibitions. He has to reprove division, but he never urges agreement by concession and compromise. He has to blame their failures, but he proposes to them no scheme of service and defines no one type of character. Even for the furtherance of the Gospel he sets up no machinery for concerted action. His final and unchanging faith is in a fellowship, manifesting not man's arrangements but God's direct, individual rule, which yet is the only perfect harmony. And he knows that harmony is not uniformity. Like the spring which has one effect in the vine-clad valley and another on the mountain-slope, one on the verge of the arctic mists and another where shining seas laugh up to sunlit skies, yet all contribute to the fullness of the earth and show it to be the Lord's, so God's Rule is ever varied but ever graciously and freely productive in human souls, while making all their work serve His eternal and infinite purpose in harmony and effectiveness.

In a fellowship of this order it is mere support of one another in error to have one belief, if it do not correspond with God's actual purpose: and even the most perfect sympathy would be vain, if it were not in accord with God's rule for realising it. But if God's Rule is for the good of His children as love measures it and by the power of love as wisdom directs it, and if this utterly changes life as we must live it and the world as we must use it, and if the Gospel is the good-news of it, how is it to be forwarded by substituting for it any rule of man? Why, indeed, should it be forwarded, unless it is equal to the task of ordering all duties and using all experiences? If God's guidance and succour is life's supreme reality, it must enable men to serve all the high ends of the spirit, by a blessed wealth of varied loyalties, in many different manifestations, while joy and peace turn service into liberty: and it cannot be that we commend it by falling back on even the best human formulas or the wisest human regulations.

Let us remember that furthering the good-news means actually getting people to live in the joy and emancipation and freedom of God's own ever present, ever active, ever blessed Rule, and that it is not furthered at all by merely imposing upon others statements about it which alter nothing either in themselves or their world. Acquiescence is nothing; discovery is everything. Pressure is vain; fear is folly; anathema brutality: for good-news, by its very nature, cannot be forced upon the mind, but must sing its way into the heart. And why should any other way of furthering it ever be thought necessary, if it is good-news of a

Rule of God, as blessed as it is secure; or any embodiment of it be thought possible except a fellowship of its own creating?

In our day few of us are borne up by the assurance of good-news of a reality which will recreate the world by planting an exhaustless joy and victorious hope in the hearts of men. With what measure of faith could we write to any of the Christian communities, and more particularly to any of the organised Churches, rejoicing in our fellowship in the furtherance of this high end? Does any high purpose stand steadily before us? Is there so much as a sure conviction that high purpose is life's meaning? Instead of being able to say that our labour is not in vain in the Lord, are we not painfully aware that even the best of it, such as the training of the young and preaching to the poor, is quite distressingly futile for any kind of furthering the Gospel?

Is it because the Rule of God is not in reality what the Gospel proclaims it to be, or only because our fellowship, not being really ordered by it, does not manifest it? What the world sees is not a great joy, springing spontaneously from a reality which, being at once a great possession and the means for possessing all else according to its divine and eternal value, unites us spontaneously in conviction, esteem and service. What it does observe is a widespread, persistent endeavour to induce every one to repeat the same form of words, in the pathetic conviction that, could it be done with united and emphatic voice, speaking in one institution with one creed and one order, it could batter a breach for the Gospel through every conceivable form of human resistance. And what the world is mostly persuaded of as the result is that the concern is not about truth, but about conventional agreement regarding a dead tradition, which a class of stupid people accepts from custom and a class of dishonest people maintains from self-interest. The only practical outcome is thought to be routine religious services and negative, merely respectable moralities, which challenge none to consider or to imitate, and under the influence of which our churches become dull clubs, not inspired brotherhoods, and our labour for ecclesiastical success, and not for a regenerated humanity and a renovated world.

This may be a total misrepresentation. But, so far as furthering the Gospel is concerned, that is not the question. The question is whether we have not given cause for it by concerning ourselves anxiously about the body of our fellowship and failing to show glad trust in the creative power of its spirit?

Nothing on this earth lives and works as mere spirit. Every truth, in particular, must fashion for itself a form of outward expression and a vehicle of organised activity. But though the soul needs a body, the body is nothing except as the expression and vehicle of the soul: and that relation of dependence we must especially in spiritual things maintain. Thus a creed is one thing when it is the expression of a common faith inspired by individual vision of one Divine reality, and quite another when it is a mere ecclesiastical formula which people do not trouble either to understand or to reject; an institution is one thing when it incorporates a spirit of brotherhood because each member of it loves his brethren in the Father of his Lord, and quite another when it is merely the work of ecclesiastical arrangement and compromise; organisation is one thing when it is the natural working of the citizens of God's Kingdom united in His service, and it is quite another when it is merely ecclesiastical machinery whereby a few persons may control the activities of the rest.

The question is whether the enormous concern of the Church with this latter kind of creed and institution and organisation has not been misdirected energy. To neglect it would be, we must admit, to neglect much that has in all ages been cultivated with zealous diligence. But did not Jesus deliberately and conspicuously neglect it, concentrating His whole effort on showing the Father? Having set men face to face with this reality, did He not stake everything on their response to it? Was not His whole programme for a new world that His disciples should be a leaven to change its unrighteousness, salt to banish its corruption, light to dispel its darkness, life to abolish its death? In short, was not the fellowship of the Kingdom for Him the one way of furthering its good-news? And if furthering the Gospel means delivering the souls of men from the power of evil, providing them with higher and more blessed possessions, transforming their desires and ambitions, regenerating their society here and giving them a sure hope of one more perfect hereafter, what can avail for it except a fellowship already in possession of these blessings?

Man has many and sore temptations actively to commit iniquity. The least of them leads into by-ways, miry and perilous and blind. Nevertheless, by the worst he may, with effort and loss and pain, return and start anew. But there is a temptation which has not even this belated and sorrowful promise. It is to call a halt where he feels himself tolerably at ease and thinks himself tolerably secure. Only as he succumbs to it does man renounce his high destiny: and the renunciation would be final and irremediable were not God's winds forever levelling his tents and God's rains forever flooding him out upon higher ground.

How often has the Church given way to this temptation, ceasing to strive for a unity in which, through the good-news of God in Jesus Christ, each one sees the same reality, drinks of the same spirit and gladly accepts as his own the same Divine rule, and seeking it instead by fixed creed, uniform organisation, and even by an ordering of recognised duties, all imposed purely from without to conserve what seems already won!

Endless labour has been spent on thus building,

on any place at which men had arrived and where they proposed to stay, a tower from which to scale the battlements of Heaven. Even when confusion of tongues fell upon them and divided their efforts, they merely blamed other people's forms of speech, and did not reflect that it might be God's way of forcing them forward into a larger world where Heaven might be near without any necessity of building up to it, and where, by its guidance, they might travel together, in one faith and one loyalty, because of the leading of the one God who is Father of all, towards nothing less than His infinite and eternal purpose. Should we not therein have both blessed peace and good-success, did we turn our hearts from man's arranging and trust the good-news of God Himself in Jesus Christ to order all our doings by uniting us in the vision of His one truth, in love to His children as we love our common Father, and in the service of love in His Kingdom of righteousness and peace and joy in His Spirit, which is the Spirit of all that, in glorious and varied harmony, is true and beautiful and holy?

Greed still debases our souls, suspicions and hatreds still rend our society, and religion still sanctions our narrow sympathies with the appearance of piety. Under new names we still cherish old distinctions little altered. German and English, Catholic and Protestant, Nigger and White, are still in substance Barbarian and Scythian, Greek and Jew, Bond and Free. Is it because the good-news of Jesus

Christ, with His fellowship with the Father and, through it, with His children, is an unreality, that these things have not in Him ceased to be? Or is it only because, as a matter of fact, we have had, even in religion, our trust in man's devices, and have not yet, in spite of our long, sorrowful experience, learned that there can be no utterly reliable news for our state except of God, and that we cannot build any better society upon a less enduring foundation than a fellowship which we enter as we live in God's truth, are one in His spirit, and serve a kingdom where He rules by teaching us that His will is also our own hearts' desire?

XXI

THE LAWS OF PRAYER

LUKE xi. 9. 'And I say unto you, Ask, and it shall be given you; seek, and ye shall find; knock, and it shall be opened unto you.'

MUCH of our Lord's teaching is very startling when we think, and is not questioned only because few people think about the familiar. This is specially true concerning most of the sayings on prayer. What of those enchanter's words which remove mountains? What even about this fixed law of receiving? Is it not refuted by the commonest experiences? We may have read of marvellous answers to petitions, and we may even have known instances. Only incredulity, it may be, could believe them accidental coincidence. But could credulity itself maintain that there is any approach in life to a general rule that what we ask we invariably receive?

By supposing our Lord to mean spiritual need, and not every imaginable want, the difficulty is made smaller. And this limitation He does seem to set. Even if we asked for a stone, He says, thinking it bread, God gives bread, not stone; while the final promise of the Holy Spirit also speaks of spiritual, not of temporal blessings. In the light of both sayings we must read the whole discourse. Yet, except that there is spiritual profit from any earnest prayer, the answer is no more according to rule in spiritual than in temporal concerns. The most unselfish petition which ever goes up into the ear of God is the strong crying with tears of a mother for her erring son. Yet we have seen sons of many prayers perish miserably, victims of their own vices. Prayer no more works spiritual than physical magic. Moral results are what we make them and not what we wish them. In this sphere also law operates as much as in the material, especially the inexorable law that whatsoever a man soweth, that shall he also reap. The most agonising supplication, either from the transgressor or from his most pious friend, will not avail to prevent the calamitous harvest of a sowing of wild oats, or, still less, to turn it into the fruitful field of the diligent. The prayer neither of penitence nor of compassion will speak any wonder-working word to save the sinner from the long and arduous and deadly conflict by which transgression must be undone and evil habit broken.

This rule of experience, moreover, is a necessity, if the Divine government is not to veer, like the weather vane, at every breath of human emotion. There, in that rule of highest wisdom, lies the real difficulty concerning prayer. To the reverent and reflecting soul this is a far greater difficulty than the mere rigidity of the laws of nature; or, if the difficulty is still with natural law, it is not as inflexible order but as the rule of a wisdom which cannot change. If God is absolutely good and absolutely wise, if He knows all with absolute knowledge and does all with absolute power, where is there place in His government for the interference of ignorant, erring, foolish mortals? God deals with us as with children, and the law which is above every law is the law of love. But must not love itself refuse to accommodate its wise purposes to our unwise desires? If God's rule is already the wisest and the best, must not love, even for our sakes, guard it from our foolish interference?

Yet, if God really deals with us as with children, might not a law of prayer itself prove to be part of this wisest and best rule? We know what stultified pomposity it is in a human parent to think himself too wise to be guided by the thoughts, or even the desires of his smallest child. But if such superiority is folly in man, would it be wisdom in God? May not the perfection of His wisdom enable Him to omit no purpose of any of His children from the working out of His own? But, in that case, among the laws of His acting there must be a law of prayer; nor could the discovery of any other law be more important for understanding His government of the world.

This law our Lord here enunciates. It is no sanction of wandering desires or worship of our own wills, but just the highest example of the great law of sowing and reaping. It sets forth three methods of God and three stages of our own prayers: and by considering them, we may see, not only how God answers prayer, but how no prayer goes unanswered.

First, you observe, prayer is spoken of as an asking in order to receive. If we ask, we receive without condition made or exception admitted. This is the first law—THE LAW OF RECEIVING.

There are doubtless definite and direct answers to prayer; and, if we asked more simply and with greater faith, we might all be surer of God's hand in the events of our lives. But we have also the highest examples to warn us not to expect, in any uniform, immediate or visible way, the thing we ask. Paul thrice besought the Lord in vain that the messenger of Satan to buffet him should depart. A still greater than Paul, even He who uttered this saying, cried, 'If it be possible, let this cup pass from me': and it did not pass. The Cross was the only answer to His prayer. It is the answer to many prayers. Perhaps no one rightly prays in Christ's name without realising that it may be the answer to any prayer.

Yet we may not say that either asked and was denied. Paul's desire to profit by all experiences was greater than his desire to choose what any experience might be. The Master's wish that God's will should be done was far above any wish to be spared any agony necessary for the doing of it. When God's will was done, for His glory and the good of man, Jesus had nothing in His heart but utter submission.

This distinction between the wish of the moment and the unwavering purpose of the life must ever be kept in mind. In the outer court of our nature, where we are influenced by the occasion and make use of words, we may utter one prayer; and, in the inner sanctuary of our unchanging aspiration, our hearts be set on another. If the former is set aside for the latter, our true prayer is not unanswered. Spoken prayer may be a very superficial asking. Prayer, as the hymn says, is 'the soul's sincere desire.' Nay, 'sincere' is superfluous. All desire is sincere. Only the utterance of it can be insincere. Every longing is a prayer; and our most effectual, fervent prayer is our strongest longing. But, if that is so, for what have you prayed? For everything, base as well as noble, you ever set your heart on.

If this be the meaning of asking, is our Lord's assertion so certainly contradicted by experience? Do we not all, in a quite amazing way, receive in the line of our desires? Many lives are a mass of conflicting desires, which, as they spring from mere changing discontent, cannot be satisfied. But, if there is one dominating desire in life, how constantly does life come in the line of it! You think of this as the mere effect of concentration, but when you seriously consider your life, do you not find very little of it exclusively the work of your own hands, and most of it sheer gift, which has marvellously come in the line of your desires, even though the fulfilment of your desire may have been far from satisfying you when it came? Is the Buddhist saying, that our lives follow our thoughts as the wheel the foot of the ox that draws the carriage, much at variance with experience? Does not God give to our asking in a way to startle and dismay, in a way to drive us to our knees, if only we would take thought of what it means, to pray God to qualify our desires by the wise purposes of His holy will?

This ennobling of our petitions is one of the most imperative ends of public prayer. In the conscious presence of God and in the fellowship of our brethren, even the prayer for daily bread may rise into a higher region of gratitude and of regard for the wants of others; intercession become a sense of common service and of the impossibility of selfish good; and, finally, with the perfect spirit of common worship, all other things we could desire be subjected to the search for the Kingdom of God and its righteousness.

But if the sanctuary is the place of better petitions, the closet of our hearts, when the door is shut upon our secret thoughts, is the place of surest answers. From thence the prayers go up continuously, concerning which it is amazingly, startlingly, even appallingly true, that whatsoever we ask we receive.

And, beyond this life, is eternity with the answers which still await our longing. Our highest aspirations alone may be its promise, but none of our desires may be wholly unanswered.

All we have willed or hoped or dreamed of good shall exist.

And though the good only may be everlasting, may not the evil also have a kind of immortality? To employ a figure used in another connection: 'as the fins of a fish foreshadow that water exists, or the wings of an eagle in the egg presuppose air,' so every longing of the heart foreshadows some kind of realisation. That is a universal law: and it is the laws of the spirit, and not of the body, which endure.

Strange mystery of the soul of man made in the image of God, strange power of his asking, strange intimacy with the working of the Eternal! To whatsoever we ask the answer is so sure that for it we need have no concern. Our one need is to be taught to ask truly in Christ's name, so that all our desires may be wholly according to the Father's love and the Father's wisdom.

But, if we receive what we ask, we do not receive it at our own time and in our own way. Yet it is not the whole truth, when we say, it is at God's time and in His way. That is not adequate, because it is not His mere pleasure which determines either His giving or His withholding. The law of receiving is suspended only by a higher law—THE LAW OF FINDING.

Suppose you were a collector of rare plants. To have one given you might be a very great pleasure, but would it afford you the same satisfaction or be your very own, as if you had found it for yourself?

The people whose soil and climate present them freely with food and warmth are not, in the end, so richly endowed as those who raise their bread from the clayey furrow and build their shelter under the biting wind. These blessings are not less, but more beneficently given, because they do not say, 'Here we are, put forth your hand and receive,' but, 'We shall be here, when you dig for us and find.' And just as little do God's spiritual gifts become less free, or less gracious, or less abundant, or less sure when they cease to say, 'Receive,' and begin to say, 'Find.'

Of nothing is this truer than the truth itself. God, we too readily assume, must speak and man simply receive. But it is not so now, and never has been. God is wiser, more patient, and, above all, more magnanimous. 'It is,' one of the Proverbs says, 'the glory of God to conceal a thing, but the honour of kings is to search out a matter.' To give this regal glory, God conceals. He would lift us up and crown us, in the glory of His own discernment, over all His works. Hence no word of His says from the skies, 'Hear and believe.' His revelation comes through human experience, through the souls that have sought and found: and it is revelation to us also as we are of their kindred and are willing to seek that we too may find.

Nor is the supreme revelation, the Word of God Himself, an exception. Even His sayings and doings are valueless, till, by seeking, we find them for ourselves anew. His truth may be the most familiar thing in life, yet have no real existence for us, even as a man might plough all his days with the gold shining in the furrow, yet die in poverty. Christ's demand still is, 'Seek and ye shall find'; and those He never fails are the seekers after God. The same is true of every gift He has to give. Never to cease to hunger and thirst after righteousness is never to fail. Even should sin prevail and vice enslave, to know our poverty and to continue to seek is to find God, and, with Him, the unsearchable riches.

In God's eyes we are rather what we seek than what we have attained. What men take us to be is often mere effect of custom, training and good influences. Only what we seek shows what in our own hearts we are, and prophesies what, in the end, we shall be. Wherefore, even more than what we ask, it is the wings of the eagle in the egg. Even in time, the best of life is finding what we seek; and, in the day when our real spiritual world disentangles itself from the fashions and shadows of time, we shall find the rest. There need be no uncertainty about finding. The one fear is that the thing we have been seeking may prove ashes for bread, wormwood for wine, corruption for life, darkness for light.

This Law of Finding, however, is limited by a still higher law, which is THE LAW OF DISCOVERING.

'Knock and it shall be opened unto you.'

This is the law which requires the long delays to which we are all subjected and by which so many are discouraged. For many weary years we may stand faced by doors which never open to our knocking. If we have accepted no denial, if delay has only enlarged our measure of blessings beyond our present knowing and increased our urgency, then we have most truly waited upon God. Such persistent knocking at the door of life's mystery is the deepest, the best attested, the most efficacious utterance of the heart, the only form of prayer wholly adequate to God's infinite and eternal purpose with the souls of men.

To knock that it may be opened unto us is more than to receive what we know we desire, and more than to find what we know we are seeking. It is the awaiting of a discovery of truth and beauty and goodness beyond all our knowing. Yet it is not a mere expectation of lighting upon, by accident, something wholly unanticipated and strange. Like all discovery, it is at once beyond our asking or our seeking yet the receiving of our heart's desire, the finding of what we have ever pursued. It is the unexpected, yet the realisation of our expectation; the strange, yet with nothing stranger in it than its familiarity. The barrier falls and blank obstruction gives way to radiant vistas, but we are still standing on the old path, and somehow it is still just the road we expected to travel.

When Kepler, after years of study, discovered the true orbit of the planets, it was a new revelation to lift up his heart in wonder and adoration, but, while it had the marvel of the unexpected, had it the strangeness of the unanticipated? Rather would it appear merely simple and beautiful and right, the natural order of his disordered ideas, the perfection he had ever followed, so fitting as to leave him amazed at ever having thought that God's way of working was different.

When, after effecting with long and vain endeavour only prose and dullness, the poet's 'thoughts in harmonious numbers move,' and the expression one with the thought rises like a perfect star on his horizon, is it not, though undreamt of, simply the realisation of all he had dreamed?

All our best possessions come to us as such discoveries. We follow a flutter of white raiment, and are suddenly confronted by the face of our guardian angel. Or in the figure of our text, after long weary years of knocking, the door, which blankly closed our vista, suddenly opens, and we are filled with the sense of wonder, yet not of strangeness, for, while it is utterly different from all we pictured, it is wholly the fulfilment of what we have loved without knowing how to desire or pursue. Thus it is with the truth which sets us free, the pardon which gives us peace, the grace which sustains our wills, the faith which encourages our hearts.

It is summed up in the greatest of all things, which is love. But love is not content merely to satisfy us, or to see us attaining merely what we know to pursue. It would make us worthy of nobler satisfaction, and would open for us doors into experiences undreamt of, which are yet the only perfect realisation of all our aspiration and all our endeavour. God, being love, has in store for us what eye has not seen, nor ear heard, nor the heart of man conceived; and we wait on His purpose as we keep knocking at the door of life's mysteries and unrealised possibilities.

All our days God is opening doors for those of us who continue knocking, but the blankest one at the end is also the widest. When it opens, it will be in the largest sense upon what it has not entered into our heart to conceive. Yet may there not be, in a still deeper sense, nothing new? Shall we not find ourselves still on the old road, with nothing altered except the opening of the gates which obstructed our vision? Life will stretch before us with a vast and hitherto unrealised meaning, but will it not also be just the old life, with its meaning the fulfilment of life's foreshadowings and its blessings the natural satisfaction of our gropings?

We shall then know that our greatest, truest, most efficacious prayers were neither our petitions for what we thought we needed, nor our reaching out after what we thought our goal, but what the Apostle calls the groanings that cannot be uttered, the ceaseless unrest for what was, in this world, ever beyond our knowing.

God keeps us waiting and dissatisfied and un-blessed, not because He would not gladly satisfy our desire and reward our seeking, but because His is a larger love which would give us a still higher possession on the better title of our own discovery. In that confidence let us pray—asking, seeking, knocking—knowing the blankest door of His seeming denial to be only the barrier that will open upon His fullest manifestation. So shall we pray, not only when we worship together in the sanctuary or kneel at our private devotions, but by a whole life of trust, of dependence, of thanksgiving, and, above all, of waiting at the door of life's mystery, which is life's prophecy and hope.